Advance Praise

"'Student centered learning' is often lauded and too seldom practiced; Plotinsky's book is both rallying call and practical, down-to-Earth guide for teachers who really want to move from 'sage on the stage' to 'guide on the side.' She shows how creating the conditions for students to take charge of their own learning involves teachers making certain challenging but absolutely doable transformations in their approach, and in a concise and engaging manner walks educators through how to make this transition. The result is a classroom that improves not only learning, but also engagement and equity."

—**David Nurenberg, PhD**, Associate Professor of Education, Lesley University, author of *"What Does Injustice Have to Do with Me?": Engaging Privileged White Students with Social Justice*

"The crux of Plotinsky's argument is central to the conversations that should be happening within every meeting in every school: how can we get out of the way of student learning? Plotinsky shares tangible ways in which we can move from being the 'sage on the stage' to the 'guide on the side' and her words are grounded in what needs to happen first: we have to target our belief systems for reflection and upgrade."

—**Casey Siddons**, Assistant Principal, Montgomery County Public Schools, Maryland, and cohost of the Ed's (Not) Dead podcast

"The power of Plotinsky's work resides in her advancing a pedagogy of motivation. If we are going to modernize schools to meet the needs of our students, if education is going to keep pace in the age of total information, it will be by developing student autonomy. Teach More, Hover Less proposes an educational paradigm shift where relationships, careful curation, flexible settings, and student choice leads to the state of flow teachers chase in dreams."

—**Christopher R. Klein**, Staff Development Teacher, John F. Kennedy High School, Maryland

teach more,
hover less

Norton Books in Education

teach more, hover less

How to
Stop Micromanaging
Your Secondary Classroom

Miriam Plotinsky

W. W. NORTON & COMPANY

Independent Publishers Since 1923

Note to Readers: Models and/or techniques described in this volume are illustrative or are included for general informational purposes only; neither the publisher nor the author can guarantee the efficacy or appropriateness of any particular recommendation in every circumstance. As of press time, the URLs displayed in this book link or refer to existing sites. The publisher and author are not responsible for any content that appears on third-party websites.

For Kenny –
who has always seen me.
I love you.

Contents

Acknowledgments   xi

Introduction   xiii

Chapter 1   Mindset Shifts: The First Stage   1

Chapter 2   Reframing Relationships: The Second Stage   21

Chapter 3   From Engagement to Investment: The Third Stage   39

Chapter 4   Choice-Based Instruction: The Fourth Stage   57

Chapter 5   Pulling It All Together: The Four Stages of
             Hands-Off Instruction   77

References   99
Index   101

Acknowledgments

None of this would be possible without the team at Norton Books in Education. To my editor, Carol Chambers Collins, whose straightforward advice has been endlessly helpful: thank you for embracing my work and believing in me. To Jamie Vincent, thank you for discovering my writing. I am also thankful to Mariah Eppes and Emma Paolini, both of whom answered every question I had with patience and cheer.

Thank you to the editors at *Edutopia* and *EdSurge* for publishing my articles on student ownership that paved the way to this book.

To my MCPS family of leaders, teachers and students: I am both fortunate and thankful that you have made my professional home so fulfilling for the past 20-plus years.

My loved ones get the worst of me when deadlines approach, and they respond by keeping everything afloat. To my loving parents, thank you for reading early chapter iterations and encouraging me. To Koby, Ayla and Dalya: I am so grateful for you three. You are my life and my hope, and the best Quarantine Crew a mother could ever ask for. And to Kenny, who read endless drafts and provided feedback so insightful that I wonder if you should explore a second career as an editor: thank you for putting all of your books aside to read mine, for being the Type-B partner in this relationship, and for being my absolute favorite person.

Introduction

Hindsight may provide insight, but it can take years of self-reflection, not to mention trial and error, before we are comfortable with our teaching identities. Those earlier, cringeworthy moments in our classrooms can be difficult to think about, but they explain so much about who we decide to become as we find our teaching voice and purpose. Personally, I have made my fair share of instructional missteps, but what bothers me more than individual instances that occurred at isolated times are the consistent and ongoing beliefs I held earlier in my career. For example, I had a sense (without any further rationale) that students were supposed to meet due dates and deadlines no matter the circumstance, which resulted in a far more rigid approach that was not responsive to student needs. After all, I had been taught as a child that meeting deadlines was important, though I never stopped to think about whether having work submitted by a particular date was more valuable than how well I understood course content.

When I became a teacher, I should have been focusing with a lot more intention and self-reflection on whether students in my classes knew that their ability to meet learning outcomes in the work they produced was a higher priority than finishing assignments on time. Instead, I appeared to place a stronger emphasis on behavior than on academic growth, and this messaging led to instructional mistakes with farther-reaching implications. In thinking about how students were tracked into courses, I believed that student behavior was an acceptable criterion for their course placements into what were perceived as more or less challenging classes; if they could just work harder or tap into more enthusiasm, students would grow. However, I did not fully realize that it is primarily the teacher's job to motivate students, nor did I take responsibility for how I looked to create a classroom space that focused on intrinsic rather than extrinsic motivational methods. To that end, while I now see tracking to be a practice that supports inequity, it took a while for me to understand that separating students into honors versus on-level courses was damaging to their academic identities, often irreparably so.

These and many other beliefs I held with or without my awareness still bother me, and I seek to rectify how I accepted so many traditional teaching tenets without question, simply because I had experienced similar systems as a student. To this day, I regret that it took me more than 10 years in the classroom to explore a new set of core teaching beliefs. For all I know, my perspective may have never changed had I not been given the chance to teach a course with an unusual feature: It was unleveled (i.e., open to students in all four high school grades) and untracked. In this class, students from almost every conceivable academic or personal background and walk of life sat in the same room together, learning and supporting one another. When I saw how natural it was for students with a range of experiences and points of view to elevate one another not in spite of but *because* of their differences, I realized that I had been wrong in thinking that grouping by perceived ability (never accurate, always limiting) was a mistake.

As cracks began to appear in some of the systems I was conditioned to think were effective, the educational house of cards I had once believed in began crumbling around me. My colleagues shared many of the same revelations I had, such as our increased awareness of implicit bias and the need to create more opportunity and access for all students. However, other parts of my journey were more individual to my teaching experience as I began to think about new ways to do my job. Some of the changes my instruction required seemed minute, but details matter. My speaking voice was often tired and scratchy at the end of the day; why was I talking so much? Were my students truly listening and benefiting from my dominance over the class, or was there a better way to reach them? Even more important, was I keeping too much hold over what was happening throughout instruction, out of the worry that if I didn't micro-manage every last aspect of the class, I would somehow lose control of the students?

Gradually, I began experimenting with ways to change how I taught. My first concrete goal has remained my number one goal: to talk less. Instead of starting each class period with a string of operational announcements that few listened to or cared about, I asked students to sign up to either develop or facilitate an activator that was aligned to a content-based theme. Suppose we were studying a work of social protest; the activator would need to connect to a related idea, such as sharing one thing we might change about the world around us. Rather than devote any length of class time to imparting even instructional information verbally at the front of the classroom, I began to create tools that students could use for self-exploration, whether that involved presenting the class with a variety of resources to read and letting them choose what to work with, or creating stations with different options, such as a small-group discussion corner or an artistic-creation space. At that point, my experience was limited to teaching English in the high school grades, where such student-centric models were less common, so I had a steeper learning curve. As I visited other teachers' classrooms in grades K–12 and learned more about stepping back, it got easier to pull instruction further and further away from a teacher-centered focus.

I have worked in different classrooms, different schools, and different roles, and with each new context, the importance of a teaching model that encourages student agency has become more urgently apparent. While earning my certification as a school administrator, I conducted focus groups for a paper on student engagement that set off another series of lightbulbs in my head. One student who described himself as "bored" in class (a common student complaint, and often nonspecific) said something I will never forget. When asked about what he did like about school, he said, "There's one class I don't skip because even though the teacher is fun like a lot of teachers, she also cares whether I learn. She wants me to get something from her class."

At that moment, I realized that while the term "warm demander" is bandied about frequently in reference to how we should approach students, I had mainly just internalized the "warm" part of the phrase without the "demander." It was not enough to make my classroom a warm and welcoming space, though that did matter. It was not enough for students to have rigorous and flexible choices with course materials, though that was also extremely important. It was essential that when students entered the classroom, they realized that my expectations for their academic success were not reflective of just my belief in their learning; my actions also had to support those beliefs through a consistent validation of who they were as learners, not just as people. That meant that I needed to work harder to align the content of the course with the needs of the specific students who sat in front of me.

But how could that happen? It sounded like an impossible standard to set, and at first, I read a lot of scholarly books and articles about differentiation in the hopes that blended instructional models would provide some answers. However, as is often the case when we try to apply theory to practice, I hit many walls. My classes were often extremely large and student need was too variable for a lot of the suggestions around Universal Design for Learning (UDL) to work with ideal effectiveness. Somewhere along the way it finally dawned on me that in order to help each student in my class on an individual basis, I would have to restructure the way I taught, once again. The components were all there: choice, agility, student-centered learning, student voice. What was missing? Then it hit me: I was still holding on to every aspect of every class with a viselike grip. I was planning (overplanning, if I'm being honest) each class down to the second, and I needed a partial reset.

That exact instant of realization is where the four stages of what in this book I'll call "hands-off" or "hover-free" were born. As teachers, we want to change weaknesses in our approach as quickly as possible, but sometimes slowing down has benefits that yield greater returns. To that end, I spent more time deconstructing my beliefs, thought about developing more meaningful relationships with students, looked at planning my lessons differently, and focused on executing instruction more effectively than I had in the past. These stages did not represent any kind of magic bullet: There is no such thing in our profession. Rather, going through a recursive process of holding up my teaching to a bright light and being willing to change what I previously held to be true made a gradual and important difference. To this day, I continue to make mistakes as I teach, be humbled, and then use even the painful moments as opportunities to grow. The outcome of progress and not perfection helps us get a little bit better as long as we continue to dedicate ourselves to helping students achieve. It is in that spirit of growth mindset that the four stages of hands-off instruction were created; we will now explore them in further detail.

The Four Stages of Hover-Free, Hands-Off Instruction

When we watch a television show or movie that takes place in an instructional setting, classroom scenes usually follow a construct that has become all too familiar. A teacher stands at the front of the room next to a board while students sit in front of them, listening (or not) to a lecture of some kind. In reality, classrooms look less like the Hollywood conception of school. Particularly in the wake of a global pandemic, our image of a classroom community in secondary education is rapidly evolving. The learning experience is no longer limited to the static setup of students occupying rows of desks with a teacher closely monitoring activities, especially with the increasing prevalence of concurrent (i.e., combining virtual and in-person) instructional models. If we cannot always be in physical proximity to our classes, it is more immediately necessary for students to be empowered to take ownership of their learning without the micromanagement of educators. The question this book explores is: How can we learn to step back and allow students more agency? Although I coach teachers from K to 12 and have taught in both elementary and secondary classrooms, this book is focused on middle and high school students. The strategies throughout this text are more suited to older students, and since my background is strongly secondary, I have had ample opportunity to both test these methods in my own classroom and observe them in action in the skillful hands of colleagues.

A hands-off classroom starts with a dynamic class community. In this construct, we leave behind exhausting hypercontrol and invite students into partnerships that both inspire learning and withstand an unhealthy degree of adult interference. This instructional process sets students up for autonomous and deep learning from any location, with powerful ripple effects that maximize our use of classroom time. In order to achieve this desirable transition, we must first understand the four stages that make it possible to gradually shift to a different instructional approach:

1. *Mindset.* We have been conditioned to believe that meaningful learning happens only in our presence. The adaptation to a dynamic classroom community cannot move forward without a mindset shift that celebrates the power of student autonomy in learning.
2. *Deeper relationships.* In an effective educational space, we establish and maintain relationships that encourage students to take risks in safe academic spaces by sending messages that both support instructional goals and appeal to a variety of learners.
3. *Planning for engagement.* It is critical not just to establish relationships and assume that engagement with learning will take care of itself; we must also take care to build on personal connections with students and engage them cognitively in the learning.
4. *Choice-based, hands-off instruction.* This stage showcases the need for facilitating learning that can occur in flexible settings and conditions with a focus on methods that can be implemented when students are working independently or without an overabundance of oversight.

These stages act as a guide to help us think about how to design learning experiences that do not necessitate our constant overinvolvement in the classroom. They also reveal the value of creating a community dynamic that frees us from micromanagement and empowers students to move away from overreliance on our approval and supervision and take charge of their learning.

While the stages often overlap, the next four chapters of this book examine each stage separately in order to provide both clarity and processing time. It is also important to recognize the gradual nature with which change occurs; after all, we should not nurture a false expectation that reading four chapters will instantly free us from helicopter teaching. As with any worthwhile professional development, it is our consistent and persistent implementation of new methods that allows us to create a classroom of shared ownership that strengthens over time. With that in mind, this book provides practical strategies for moving through the process of creating a hands-off classroom that can be applied in classrooms right away. Before we get into how to use this book with more specificity, let us first think about the connection between theory and practice, particularly as it relates to applied research in secondary education.

Theory Versus Practice

From the moment we decide to become teachers, laypeople come at us with all kinds of advice, much of it unsolicited. It seems that because most individuals have at one time or another been in a classroom as students, they feel as though they possess some claim to instructional expertise. Those of us who dedicate so much of ourselves to honing the art of teaching, however, know better. Teaching is an art, one that is broken down into endless parts, rebuilt afresh each new school year, and refined with careful dedication over a period of many years. We may be highly self-critical in our line of work, but that does not mean we appreciate the input, well-meaning or otherwise, of individuals who have no firsthand teaching experience.

At the same time, it can also be difficult to find useful professional development from education experts, whether they are independent consultants, school leaders, or teaching colleagues. If we cannot take new-found knowledge and use it practically in our classroom, the relevance of a training experience often diminishes or disappears entirely. As teachers, we are also a notoriously difficult audience to impress when it comes to any continuing education experience, probably because we pour so much energy and attention into our own classes and pedagogical growth. How many times have we sat in a training session grading papers surreptitiously as someone presented a slideshow at the front of the room? How many times have we thought, "If I taught the way this presentation is being given to me, I would have a failing teaching evaluation," and doubted the worth of whatever was being shared? And how many times have we picked up a book or article about our profession only to find it dense, hypothetical, and lacking in useful application?

Teaching is a verb. It is through action that we make progress, whether that describes what happens during instruction or accounts for the important planning time that occurs both before and after class. I have never met a teacher who enters the classroom with the express goal of mediocrity; we want to do the very best for our students. Traditionally, the way we elevate our practice is by learning from those we trust the most to guide us: our colleagues. Most crucially, we want to include students in the key group we consult when we seek to become better at our jobs. Students are our most important clientele and are particularly suited to help us grow because, unlike our colleagues, they actually sit in our classrooms and have firsthand knowledge of both what works and what could make the classroom environment even more conducive to their achievement.

We all read education books differently. Some of us read the chapters in order, while others (I am one of these people) like to flip around according to personal whim. However you choose to access the information in this text, my suggestion is to read Chapters 2, 3, 4, and 5 in order for the sake of clarity. The four stages of hands-off instruction are presented sequentially to more easily communicate a specific shared ownership classroom approach. However, while the stages should initially be reviewed in the order presented, they can be implemented recursively and in any sequence once we begin to translate the ideas into our practice. Once again, the reality of making a theory actionable lies in our ability to apply what we learn to our classrooms right away. That immediacy is so important whenever we seek to grow professionally, which is why this book is full of tools, resources, and strategies for experimenting with a classroom that is free of micromanaged instruction. This book is also strongly anecdotal, but it should be noted that the stories shared in this text are fictional. The situations described are ones that will ring true to any seasoned educator, but the specific events are fictional and the teachers and students contained in the narratives are composites, not real people.

We may begin the process of hover-free teaching in consideration of our own individualized professional needs, but we may also wish to approach the content of this book in the spirit of collaboration. Anytime we engage in professional learning, our ultimate mastery of new pedagogical goals is heightened by the work we do with our colleagues. Teaching styles certainly vary, but that is a benefit rather than a pitfall of working with others; it is those very differences in our methods that enable us to examine and elevate our own practices with more insight, more enthusiasm, and the empathy of others who are with us on our professional journeys.

The phrase "helicopter parent" is culturally ubiquitous, but perhaps we have not given as much thought to the idea of helicopter *teaching*. The more we seek to increase our hypervigilance in every aspect of instruction, the more we risk not just exhausting ourselves but also failing to meet the needs of our students. In a society that increasingly relies on varied modes of teaching (technological expertise and proficiency with culturally responsive teaching come to mind), not to mention flexible learning locations in the wake of an increased prevalence of virtual teaching post-2020, it is pretty much impossible to supervise every minute detail of our classes effectively. The solution is to increase student agency in our classes by achieving a hands-off teaching model: As discussed, the one in this book applies specifically to students in secondary education.

The Research Gap: Looking to Higher Education

Why even look at distance-learning models in higher education? For one thing, the lack of research about virtual teaching and learning in grades K–12 until the year 2020 necessitates that we look at what does exist, rather than dwelling on what does not. More urgently, the connection between remote learning models and a hands-off teaching approach is one that reflects the time in which we live. While we would like to think that all secondary educational experiences will remain within cinder-block structures, that is not a realistic expectation. Our eyes have been opened to learning settings that exist beyond classroom walls, and the old adage is absolutely true: You can't go back. Now that we know how to conduct our classes at a distance and leverage digital technology to meet challenges we were unable to address in the past, online learning (to a degree, anyway) is here to stay.

To embrace a model of teaching that removes so much of the traditional conception of teacher presence, we should begin by thinking about how we educate students both near and far. How much research specific to the middle and high school years exists in relation to teaching from flexible learning spaces, which are increasingly located online? In March of 2020, the closing of in-person instruction during a global pandemic necessitated a quick pivot to virtual learning across all school grades. Since then, the realization that online learning will remain a factor in secondary education has resulted in an urgent need for research-based practices that support agility in terms of both our location and our pedagogy. At present, the existing recommendations for distance-learning strategies that empower student agency are mainly isolated to higher education, and as we might imagine, these methods do not translate as effectively to younger students.

Having said that, we can use some of the research conducted for older students to inform our own decisions about how to approach the future of teaching, which is looking less static and more reliant on remote-learning options. The Community of Inquiry framework, a model for online lesson design developed at the University of Alberta (Garrison et al., 2000), outlines the necessity of three "presences" for online learning: social, cognitive, and teaching. The social presence is about how we build connections with our students, the cognitive presence involves our thinking around how students engage with content, and the teaching presence is all about our implementation of meaningful instruction. While these three presences are extremely relevant in both middle and high schools, they were created specifically for online lesson design.

For the purpose of making a flexible, student-centered process more relevant and applicable to secondary education, the four stages of hover-free instruction in this book are tailored for a younger, precollege audience. We have to think about how we intentionally encourage preadolescents and adolescents to take academic risks in a safe learning space. Simple rapport on its own will not lead to increased student achievement. Our planning process for instruction must include voice and choice for adolescent students, or we will not successfully engage the majority of the class.

The first stage of the hands-off process is all about how we as educators frame our teaching. How aware are we of our own core educational beliefs, and how does that play into how we do our jobs each day? Before we rush forward in our zeal to increase student agency in our classrooms, we must take the necessary time to consider our own teaching mindset. As with any meaningful process of change, we have to slow down and get our thoughts in order before implementing a plan.

Before We Begin

Before we head into Chapter 1, which explains the first stage of shifting our mindset, there is one short anecdote I would like to share that exemplifies the power of hands-off teaching. Years ago, I had the privilege of coteaching with one of the most highly skilled teachers I have ever encountered. Her energy was unflagging; her positivity and hope for students emanated from her very core. It was no accident that her students understood what she expected of them and rose to meet very clear standards. In its execution, her class was seamless. One day, after I had been struggling with a student we both found challenging, I asked her a question that had been on the tip of my tongue, one that finally formed into words: "How do you give this job 100% every day? You never seem to get tired or discouraged."

She shook her head at me. "I get discouraged all the time, but I don't dwell on it. Instead, I turn my frustration into something that I can use. If I'm too tired at the end of the day, that means I did too much and students didn't do enough. I need to give some of that responsibility right back to them."

Though I never forgot what she said, it took years for her statement to sink in fully. As teachers, we hold the power to shape and reshape our classrooms into what we consider to be an ideal state. Our vision of what that looks like changes from year to year, and that is the fundamental privilege of teaching: that we can be agile enough to keep getting better, and to keep remodeling our classrooms in the way that best serves our students. In my colleague's case, she learned that giving students agency was the best way to maintain her own positive energy as a teacher. The journey to internalizing that reality rather than just seeing it as a hypothetical starts with how we see our teaching role as it shifts time and time again. While we want to empower our students, the process begins and ends with teachers. Let's start by exploring the importance of mindset.

teach more, hover less

CHAPTER 1

Mindset Shifts: The First Stage

Mindset is the most powerful determinant of our success. If we do not confront possible contradictions between what we believe students can achieve and how our actions reflect our beliefs, we cannot make student agency a reality. For that reason, the first stage to accomplishing hands-off instruction depends upon shifting the way we think about teaching. We can then apply what we learn from self-reflection to actionable steps.

Letting Go of Helicopter Teaching

Watching a new teacher in action can tell us so much about the underlying expectations that we hold upon entering the teaching profession, not to mention what we cling to unconsciously in the years that follow. Several years ago, I observed the class of a promising rookie teacher with whom I met for regular coaching sessions. Throughout the class period, he was engaged in a particularly painful process. Every time students became rowdy, he would hold up his hand and wait for students to imitate his gesture, with the expectation that once all hands were raised, the room would be quiet. Instead, the room became even noisier. Agitated, the teacher proceeded to alternately threaten and cajole until things eventually settled down. Clearly fearful that his teaching observation would not meet standard, the teacher spent the remainder of the class period batting from one side of the room to the other like a manic housefly, hovering over his students in a losing game of whack-a-mole. When he addressed off-task behavior in one place, a group of students across the room would begin losing focus. As one might imagine, nobody learned much of anything that day. Watching him brought up a lot of uncomfortable memories of my own struggles with similar challenges at the beginning of my career.

In our post-observation conference, the teacher was beside himself with worry and frustration. "Nobody ever gets anything done unless I am literally standing right next to them," he said. "I can't turn my back, even for a second."

"And when you are right next to them?" I asked. "Does the work get done?"

The teacher froze as the reality of the situation suddenly became clear. The truth was that no matter how much he helicoptered over his students, micromanaging their every move, the class did not make much progress. His idea of control, which depended upon the constant goal of maintaining proximity to students as they worked, did not yield any desired results. So many of his best efforts were wasted in one clear, unspoken message: He lacked confidence in his class to do anything without his interference.

"So," I said, "what would happen if you just backed off?"

"Backed off?" he repeated. "But they wouldn't learn anything. They would start jumping out of the windows or throwing things at one another."

"Maybe," I said, "or maybe not. It really depends on how you set them up for success. But one thing is certain: You will keep hitting walls if you don't change your mindset."

Those of us who dedicate our lives to teaching are often conditioned to believe that the most meaningful learning happens only in our presence, often with an intense degree of hovering. This heavy-handed approach takes responsibility for learning out of students' hands as adults take too much control over the visible thinking in the room. Consider a traditional class discussion, built around the teacher's overly specific expectations. Perhaps the daily lesson involves a conversation about feminism in *The Great Gatsby*. The teacher is animated, talking excitedly about Daisy

Buchanan, walking around the room as 28 students attempt to follow her train of thought. Every time the teacher starts a sentence and points at a student to finish it, that student has to express the teacher's thought, or the answer is considered wrong. At the end of class, if the teacher has heard enough "right" answers, she thinks that the class has been successful. "What a good day," she reflects. "They were with me today." Conversely, if not enough students verbally affirm the teacher's thoughts satisfactorily, she thinks, "Ugh. They obviously didn't do the reading assignment."

Many traditional teaching models necessitate not just the presence but also the micromanagement of the teacher. If we cannot control every aspect of a student's expected response to our class, we somehow fail. If we cannot build students in our own image, we must be doing something wrong. After all, we were successful students and our teachers controlled us. Why not repeat the same teaching style and assume it works?

But wait. Did helicopter teaching work for past generations any more than it works for students today? Our awareness of inequitable educational systems is more heightened than in the past, especially now, which at the time of this writing is in the recovery phase of a global pandemic. If we pay attention, we will realize that countless so-called failing students in days gone by fell prey to being micromanaged. At the time, they were labeled as underachievers and they may even have dropped out of school, and the fault was considered to be theirs. We know better now: However unintentionally, we failed students and not the other way around. And if we really reflect upon our own educational experiences, we most likely did not enjoy being overly controlled either, even if we did learn to play the teacher's game.

In thinking about the benefits of a hands-off teaching lens, it is important to differentiate classroom management from micromanagement. The topic of classroom management gets plenty of attention, mainly because we are fearful that we will lose control over our students and not be able to teach. While nurturing that fear early in our careers, many of us become prone to a much bigger problem: micromanagement. When we try to anticipate every move our students will make, we not only limit spontaneity and autonomy; we also remove any chance that our classroom will become a dynamic community of learners that can respond with agility to desired outcomes, and we imprison ourselves in a vicious cycle of helicoptering over students who are conditioned to become too reliant on us. Truly strong instructional practice fulfills the goal of building student capacity to learn without creating codependency between the teacher and students.

What would our classrooms look like if we consciously decided on a purposeful, hover-free approach to teaching that allowed the class to seemingly run itself? It might sound like a pipe dream, but with a change in perspective, teachers and students can learn to flip the script that has made widespread independent learning an unreachable goal. The first stage of achieving a beautifully self-run classroom lies in shifting our mindset away from helicopter teaching. From a practical standpoint, it can be challenging to address core beliefs and be inspired to adjust our mindset, but confronting ideas head-on and challenging preconceived ideas allows us to invest in the all-important philosophy of teaching more, and hovering less.

Examining the Meaning of Urgency

Urgency is a significant source of interference when it comes to hands-off teaching. So many of our instructional decisions are based on the perception of what has to happen *right now*, but our priorities are often flawed because they are time bound rather than grounded in thoughtful decisions about learning. As a result, we tighten our resolve to cover the curriculum and get business done, and we rarely look back and reflect upon whether the pressure we exert on ourselves and students is doing any good. As one of my teaching friends puts it, "Your urgency is not my urgency." Why should students feel any differently when we tell them what to do, and when we never stop pestering them to fit into an instructional mold that values compliance over contemplation?

Not Everything Can Be Controlled

When the COVID-19 pandemic hit and classes became virtual on zero notice, I began working with teachers online as they struggled to reach their students from a distance. One of them, a language arts teacher, found herself grappling with a noticeable loss of instructional time. Instead of seeing students four times weekly for between 45 and 90 minutes, she now saw them only twice a week for about 40 minutes at best. "I don't know what to do," she said. "There is no time to get projects done, so I just make them write when we are together and then I pull them into breakout rooms for conferences or look at what they're writing on their shared documents. But they aren't finishing anything and this assignment should have been completed already. I have no idea what else I can try. I'm pushing so hard as it is."

"When you check up on their work constantly, does that make them more productive?" I asked. "Do they write more, or produce better content?"

"Not really," she admitted. "And that's the problem. How much more can I nag? I can't physically be there with them to make them do it. If we were in the building together, I could at least grab them in the hallway and pull them into my classroom to work with me during lunch. I can't even do that now."

"But suppose this pandemic continues," I said. "Or even suppose it doesn't, but that as we become increasingly reliant on technology, we see students physically less and less. If the only trick we have up our sleeves is to stand over them and make them do it, that won't be sustainable. In fact, I doubt it works super well even in the building. It sounds exhausting. So what else can we do? Any ideas?"

She hesitated, lost in thought. "No ideas per se, but a question. How important is it that they finish this story they're working on? You used to teach English. What would you do?"

When she asked that question, I realized that in order to believe in a hands-off classroom, this teacher had to first buy into the concept by getting a sense of what it looked like. Without a way to model the process physically, a detailed description would have to suffice. Otherwise, her mindset would remain trapped in the same undesirable world of micro-managed learning. To make the process more relatable, the hands-off scenario I shared with her exemplified a class that did a lot of writing, and it was from my own experience:

> *Years ago, the creative writing teacher at the school where I was working moved on, providing an opening for a new instructor. I had no teaching background in creative writing; all I knew was*

that it was a class free of curriculum restrictions and standard-
ized tests. When I went to my department chair and begged for
the class, I did so with very little idea of what I was asking for.
What followed was a semester of alternating panic and exhil-
aration as, for the first time, I navigated teaching a class that
had no curriculum map. Having been a rules-driven teacher for
my entire career, I felt as though I had thrown myself into the
uncharted territory of letting students decide what they wanted
to write and what the class meant to them. The class was too
unstructured for someone as organized as I was. Sure, the kids
were enjoying themselves, but were they deriving any other bene-
fit from being in the class? In those first few months, I alternated
between joy at reading what teenagers could create when given
the freedom and worry that I wasn't actually teaching them any-
thing. In fact, when a student came to me and said, "I don't know
if my writing has gotten any better," her words played into my
deepest teaching insecurities.

It was difficult to stay the course and not helicopter over the
class, but a few months went by and something magical began
to happen. With the freedom to write what they pleased without
my interference, kids began to blossom in front of me. A quiet
boy who never made eye contact with anyone wrote a brilliant
short story that thrilled everyone. From that moment on, he was
a hero. He took my class for multiple years, becoming a confi-
dent and insightful writer. Another student, a girl struggling with
recovery from drug addiction, spent the first month of my class
scrolling through her social media feed and ignoring everyone.
I was tempted to push her harder, but I held back. Slowly, she
perked up and began listening to students share their writing.
She picked up her pen. Bit by bit, she wrote about her lack of
academic identity and how she would never go to college. Even-
tually, she found her voice and became a leading editor of the
school newspaper. (adapted from Plotinsky, 2019)

As the years passed, I honed those early "aha" moments and successes
into a more clearly defined philosophy of hover-free teaching. While the

idea of stepping back might seem controversial, the first priority in a self-run classroom has nothing to do with content or learning outcomes. Rather, to achieve a classroom that relies in large part on students to drive the learning, the teacher must build and exhibit continuous trust in all members of the class to be partners in a community. Achieving that shift starts with our own mindset about our role as teachers and allows us to embrace a process that looks a little fluffy initially from a pedagogical perspective, but that begins to show dividends after just a few short weeks.

It should also be noted that while the example from my writing class pertains to an elective course, the same teaching approach works for all courses, including those that are accountable for meeting core content standards. The hands-off approach does not seek to change the "what" of curriculum goals; instead, shifting the mindset away from micromanage-ment has a significant impact on the "how" behind student investment in learning, as well as on the ability of teachers to facilitate learning with less stress and more ease. For example, math classes traditionally begin with the teacher demonstrating a problem or concept. What if students had a few minutes to collaborate before the teacher provided instruction so they could formulate ideas or questions about the task? The act of giving the class an opportunity to engage with content on their own terms not only results in heightened student agency; it also reveals what students know so far and gives the teacher data that provides a more accurate entry point for approaching learning outcomes.

The language arts teacher was intent on one priority: getting the work done in a challenging virtual setting. Her task-oriented focus was so intense that students not only resisted working on their writing assign-ment; they also received a clear (though unintentional) message that she did not trust them to write their stories. After all, from their purview, why else was she constantly checking up on them? Without realizing it, the teacher was treating a writing project like a burden, focusing mainly on the due date rather than on the potential benefits of the project. The inflexibility of a due date was clearly the first order of business, not the goal of building written expression. The teacher's hovering also served to communicate her lack of faith in the class to do the work undisturbed. To change that pattern, she would need to step back. When we surrender rigidity and learn to trust our kids, we realize how little control we have to begin with, and how much agency we are stifling.

Moving From Micromanagement to Trust

Does our teaching require lock-step compliance? Or does it promote the academic freedom that comes with critical thinking? The more we can steer instruction toward the latter and away from helicopter teaching, the better we are able to examine outdated priorities around the urgency of due dates and focus instead on learning objectives. We will also create a classroom structure that is far less stressful for ourselves. Going back to the story of the struggling language arts teacher, she arrived at a key aspect of creating a successful hands-off classroom: showing belief in our students by letting them take control over at least a portion of the class. In our conversation, we decided that for the next few weeks of school, the teacher would share daily thought-provoking or engaging writing activators at the start of class. Students would have the opportunity to jot down ideas for a few minutes and then share their thoughts for as long as they liked. If the prompt was, "Write about your name without stopping for six minutes," the teacher would open the floor, sit back and see what happened. If the conversation veered off track, she would let that occur. If the discussion lasted for the entire instructional period, that was also fine. If students were hesitant to verbally share their ideas, she would provide some low-risk alternatives (such as writing one thought in the chat box), but she would not push harder to achieve her own idea of a successful outcome. In short, the teacher would take a few steps back, listen to her students, and see what results that lack of interference yielded.

The through line that holds steady in a hands-off teaching approach is *trust*. Whether that translates into teachers trusting their students to be equal partners in the classroom community, students trusting that their teachers believe in them, or everyone trusting a process that relies on a lessening of controlling behavior, it is the underlying trust that allows us to shift our mindset away from micromanagement. One simple example of a classroom product that reflects this mutual trust is the daily agenda. Typically, teachers build the itinerary for each day on their own and present it to students at the start of a class period. Unfortunately, in our pursuit of clarity and structure, a traditional class agenda lacks student ownership. Suppose that instead of delivering an agenda each day as a fixed element, we took some time toward the end of class to work on pieces of that plan together with our students. For example, if my plan for the day involved learning about key events in the Roaring Twenties and we had only just begun to discuss Prohibition, I could show students a partly filled-out agenda for the next day and ask some questions, such as: Where should we put our continuation of this learning? What elements of Prohibition should we focus on? Is there an activity we could do to explore this topic more, either on your own or in groups? As students shared their learning preferences for the next day, we could sketch out the plan together, both increasing the mutual trust in the classroom and decreasing any micromanagement on my part. Note that I would still control some pieces of the agenda; after all, I am still the teacher. However, I would have sent the message to students that their contributions matter and that they also control aspects of our process.

As we begin to think about shifting our mindset away from micromanagement and toward trust, we may also wish to become more attuned to possible indicators of helicopter teaching. The list of look-fors in Figure 1.1 is a starting point for reflection.

While the look-fors above are phrased in a way that is more absolute or extreme than is realistic for many of us, they still point to characteristics that are often inherent in teacher mindset. To use this list, we should go through each item and check off any indicator that contains some degree of truth. When we are finished, if we have even five boxes checked off, that may set off a few tinkling bells. If we have checked more than half, those bells should probably be considered enormous Liberty Bell–sized clangs of warning. While it might be tempting to tackle the list in its entirety, it is important to undergo the process of addressing our mindset incrementally. One deceptively complex question to begin with is: How do we *really* feel about our students?

To quote renowned educator Rita Pierson, "Kids don't learn from people they don't like." Beyond that, they don't learn from people who discourage their independence, show little trust, and try to think for them. Similarly, teachers who feel burdened to do all the work for students

FIGURE 1.1   LOOK-FOR LIST: I MIGHT BE A MICROMANAGER IF . . .

☐   I plan each part of my class down to the minute, and I never stray from that plan.

☐   I have a tendency to overplan my classes; we always have too much to do.

☐   I panic about getting through the curriculum.

☐   My classroom is always neat and organized.

☐   Overall, my students learn quietly; I dislike a lot of commotion.

☐   I can tell what students need to learn. My teaching intuition is strong.

☐   If I do not watch my students, they tend to veer off-task.

☐   As much as students enjoy a fun activity or unstructured learning time, it always goes off the rails.

☐   I teach bell to bell. We begin the minute the bell rings, and I do not stop until it is time to leave.

☐   Of all the seating arrangements, I prefer teaching in rows to lessen noise and distraction.

☐   I hold my students to high expectations, and those who do not meet those expectations tend to be less successful.

☐   Differentiation is nearly impossible; it sounds nice, but it doesn't work.

☐   I plan lessons on evenings and weekends, and sometimes I am only about a week ahead of the game.

☐   I love my students, but they do not take responsibility for their work.

☐   I try to be absent rarely because my students need me to be with them.

☐   Teaching is exhausting and it feels like a constant survival game.

☐   Unless I run a tight ship, my students take advantage of me.

☐   As much as I love my job, it is just not sustainable in the long term.

rarely have time and space to reflect upon their own practice. Even if early attempts to step back from micromanagement are met with dubious results, keep trying and students will eventually understand that they are being given the opportunity to influence their learning space, whether that happens in a classroom or beyond. We may also want to pay attention to how a gradual release of helicoptering affects both teaching methodology and inner well-being. In the case of the language arts teacher, she spent two weeks prioritizing a student-led writing activity and discussion at the start of each class. Gradually, as the students got to know one another better in their new virtual spaces, the overall atmosphere of the class improved, and the teacher was able to accomplish more with the group as she moved through the stages of creating a hands-off learning environment, starting with a mindset shift.

Laying the Groundwork

It is neither realistic nor productive to assume that we will suddenly experience a mindset shift toward hands-off teaching. For that reason, the way we use our digital tools to determine our needs has to reflect honest thinking; we need to explicitly challenge ourselves to determine how we feel about the idea of micromanagement in teaching. Figure 1.2 is a quiz to help analyze just how micromanaged your current teaching style might be. If you're doing this quiz on your own while reading this book, the questions are a valuable tool for self-reflection. If your teaching team is doing the quiz together, the group can look for patterns across the team that may influence instruction on a larger scale.

There is no exact science to interpreting the results of this quiz in terms of data analysis. However, we can make inferences based on how well we know ourselves as well as on what patterns emerge. To analyze the results of the quiz, begin by seeing if your overall responses indicate a letter with the highest occurrence. The "A" category points to strong micromanagement tendencies with responses that are crafted around a viewpoint that correlates with a teacher-centric perspective. Responses in the "B" range have been designed to reflect a more student-centered approach and therefore highlight practices that are closer to being hands-off. Responses in the "C" category reveal some potential red flags around

FIGURE 1.2   MINDSET QUIZ

DIRECTIONS: Circle the answer that most closely describes your teaching style.

QUESTION 1: When class begins each day, my students:
- A) Wait for me to get them started.
- B) Have an activity or process they start on their own.
- C) Take a few minutes to settle down and chat.

QUESTION 2: If I have a planned absence, my process looks most closely like:
- A) The substitute is given highly detailed plans and related resources (handouts, materials, etc.) to distribute to students.
- B) Students already have what they need as part of ongoing learning; the substitute is there mainly as an adult authority figure.
- C) I just leave a movie for everyone to watch, or leave plans that say students can work on whatever they'd like.

QUESTION 3: If I need to step out of the room:
- A) I worry that my students will lose focus on the task.
- B) I am confident that my students will continue to work effectively.
- C) I realize that some students will work but the majority will not, and it doesn't bother me.

QUESTION 4: When I think about meeting curriculum goals, I feel that:
- A) Students need to be given the outcomes, and then they can meet them with my instruction.
- B) With my guidance, students have the ability to set goals for learning growth and achieve them.
- C) Every student has different needs, so I teach the parts of the curriculum that seem to meet the needs of the group the most.

QUESTION 5: The ownership of building an effective classroom community sits with:
- A) Mainly the teacher.
- B) The teacher and students.
- C) Ownership isn't really part of the equation.

SHORT-ANSWER QUESTION:
In one sentence, please share your most salient core belief about education.

our belief in student capacity to learn, as well as some significant gaps in pedagogy for effective teaching and learning.

If quiz results lean heavily toward one letter, that may be significant, though each individual is different and should therefore interpret any responses in conjunction with self-reflection. If responses indicate gray areas (i.e., a mix of responses among the letters), that provides ample opportunity to think about what each answer means. Suppose that I leave highly detailed substitute plans, and therefore respond to Question 2 with "A." At the same time, I answer Question 5 about student ownership with "B." That cognitive dissonance may point to a discrepancy between my beliefs and actions, and I might choose to confront my practices around how I set up my classroom for success in my absence by looking more carefully at the lesson plans I design for substitute teachers.

Each of the quiz questions addresses individual beliefs and philosophies about the capacity of students to learn without being overly controlled. When filling out this quiz, we should try to think honestly about our feelings; for that reason, the results can remain private. It is quite possible that in answering these questions, we may come to some uncomfortable conclusions about our own approach to teaching. This outcome is completely normal and should be celebrated as a sign of profound self-discovery.

In addition, looking at the quiz results will likely require a lot of thought and possible discussion; ideally, we should try to brainstorm some possible solutions to our challenges so that we do not wind up admiring the problem without addressing action steps. For the one short-answer question about core beliefs, this reflective opportunity can also provide us with the chance to think about how personal educational philosophy connects to the mindset of helicopter teaching versus trust in students. What really matters with the quiz is that we take the time to think frankly about our perceptions around hover-free teaching and any related frustrations, approaches, or beliefs. The quiz is simply a tool that helps to compile the information efficiently and has the added benefit of being able to be completed individually or at a team meeting. Overall, the main purpose of this activity should be at the fore: to help us think more profoundly about the "why" behind letting go of micromanaged classrooms.

Challenging Current Beliefs

Anyone who has ever gotten mired in a circular argument knows that changing another person's outlook can be a Sisyphean task. Even more complex is the process of changing our own minds and learning to see what we previously held as truth in a completely different light. In order to begin the process of achieving a hands-off teaching approach, it is important to look unflinchingly at our beliefs in both our own practice and in the ability of our students to shoulder more responsibility. The best way to begin this self-exploration is through reflection, either on our own or with a group of colleagues. There are benefits to both; if we work on our beliefs individually, we are more likely to be brutally honest with ourselves. If we work with colleagues, we have the benefit of group support and thought partnership. Regardless, the professional-growth activity presented in this section is designed to open up new possibilities for approaching our classes even as we acknowledge that shifting mindset is not something that typically occurs, epiphany-like, in one moment. Like most valuable growth experiences, truly adopting the ideas outlined in this book takes time.

The challenge of changing the way we look at our practice requires opportunities for professional growth. When we exhibit leadership in our capacity as teachers by guiding either the learning of colleagues or ourselves, we have the power to get the ball rolling on mindset shifts around micromanagement. The activity shared below should be explored by those of us who are closest to classroom practice; that makes the work more meaningful for anyone who may feel that traditional professional developers are too far removed from the classroom to be helpful. If it is not possible to do this activity as a teaching team, anyone reading this book for individualized professional growth can benefit from the exercises and questions, perhaps even more so depending on learning style. Like our students, many of us benefit more from working out ideas and concepts on our own before working with others.

The hallmark of a high-caliber, professional-growth experience lies in how useful we find the learning to be. Whenever I undergo any kind of learning experience, my operative question is: Does this training give me something I can use in class tomorrow? If the answer is no, then there is no perceived benefit. For that reason, when we work around the goal of shifting mindset, we have to think about how to effectively engage in challenging beliefs. Without a doubt, the most difficult part of working with mindset is simply that most of us are naturally resistant to change. When we address our beliefs about education, we must do so with the knowledge that any true shifts in perspective are likely to be accepted gradually. To that end, starting the process with an activity focused around commonly held myths about teaching that are centered on helicoptering kicks off our learning about mindset shifts around micromanagement. The activity not only addresses how to make our own teaching lives more productive and less stressful but also taps into building the collective power of an entire classroom community by trusting students to drive the learning. Figure 1.3, a chart that small groups can interact with collaboratively or that you can complete on our own, organizes ideas about myth versus mindset.

This chart is designed to address the process of shifting teacher mindset away from micromanaged classrooms. The left-hand column openly states beliefs that we commonly hold, either consciously or unconsciously, about our educational approach. As the directions at the top indicate, this activity works either individually or in small groups to shift the statements away from a controlling mindset into a hands-off perspective. When filling out the chart, we see statements that are clearly polarized in the left-hand column. The reflective power it takes to "flip" the mindset myth results in agile, critical thinking about our practice. The act of brainstorming mindset shifts is an instrumental part of beginning to embrace a new perspective. Furthermore, the blank spaces at the bottom of the chart offer us the freedom to do what we are being encouraged to learn about: to take control of our own ideas and not be guided forcefully by another person. When we engage in this exercise, we can see theory translating into action, even after just a few minutes of reflection.

The responses on this chart tend to vary widely based on our experiences. Figure 1.4 shares just a few examples of responses that teachers have given while doing this activity.

Clearly, this activity prompts ideas for further exploration. While many of the above "mindset shifts" might not be solutions, they are an important first step to recognizing helicopter teaching behaviors so that we can begin to make thoughtful and gradual modifications to practice.

FIGURE 1.3   CHART ACTIVITY: MINDSET MYTHS

HOW TO USE:

Read each myth listed below and think about what it means. Then, develop and record some alternate teaching practices that shift the mindset away from micro-management and controlling behavior.

TIP: If working collaboratively, work individually at first, and then consider engaging in discourse about the chart.

MINDSET MYTH	SHIFT THAT MINDSET!
If students are to accomplish anything, a teacher must be in close proximity for support.	Example: Students will work effectively with tasks that are engaging and clear, regardless of the teacher's proximity.
Students cannot accurately determine their own learning needs.	
For students to understand a concept, the teacher must first model the concept and provide a sample of a desired product.	
It is impossible for students to learn without constant monitoring and oversight in the form of check-ins or grading.	
The majority of meaningful learning occurs in a classroom; students have limited capacity to grow away from that space.	
Students who are talking to one another are almost certainly off-task.	
If the teacher is absent from work and a substitute is supervising, the day has essentially been a waste for student learning.	
Create your own myth.	

FIGURE 1.4   SAMPLE OF RESPONSES TO MINDSET MYTHS CHART

MINDSET MYTH	SHIFT THAT MINDSET!
If students are to accomplish anything, a teacher must be in close proximity for support.	☐ I might need to be in proximity to deliver specific parts of instruction, but I don't need to be hands-on for everything. ☐ My students sometimes work better when I let them be. ☐ I don't work well when someone keeps watching me. Maybe there's a balance between checking in and helicoptering?
Students cannot accurately determine their own learning needs.	☐ When I ask students what they are unsure about, their answers are typically spot-on. ☐ I make a lot of assumptions about what kids know, but do I have data to support my intuition?
For students to understand a concept, the teacher must first model the concept and provide a sample of a desired product.	☐ Maybe if I let kids look at a new idea or concept first and tell me what they see, I'll have a better idea of where to start with my teaching. ☐ I've noticed that when I share samples, students copy the sample instead of doing more creative work. ☐ Modeling can be good, but it can also be limiting. Is there a balance?
It is impossible for students to learn without constant monitoring and oversight in the form of check-ins or grading.	☐ I can provide feedback without a grade, and maybe students can also give one another feedback without my interference. ☐ Maybe instead of trying to be everywhere at once, I can think of better ways to check in that are less intrusive and more doable.
The majority of meaningful learning occurs in a classroom; students have limited capacity to grow away from that space.	☐ Kids can learn anywhere if I provide the groundwork; I have a student who listens to podcasts for my class when he's on the bus and headed to work and then we have amazing conversations either in class or in our online discussion board. ☐ I would like to be more strategic about how I use my physical classroom space for learning, since so much of what we do is not really limited to anything physical.

If it is possible to do this activity collaboratively, we should encourage one another to be additive rather than repetitive. For example, a colleague might share that a mindset shift about students needing to learn in the classroom only is that students are able to access meaningful learning in multiple ways. The next person might want to address that same myth and can expand upon the discussion with some strategies that might make the process easier, like flipping the classroom. As each person shares, teammates can jot down ideas that resonate so that everyone has the chart to keep as a resource. It is important to understand that building a self-run classroom model is a process and a focus of ongoing professional growth. The chart allows us to begin thinking about mindset shifts, but ongoing reflection is likely needed to determine the longer-term impact of the activity.

Momentum: Moving Forward

Whenever I work with teachers on making improvements to practice, my focus begins with educational beliefs rather than teaching skills. Most of us want to be effective and are willing to embrace new methods to improve. Changing beliefs, however, is a completely different animal. In an ideal school building, we would move toward hands-off teaching with enthusiasm both about our ability to change practice and about faith in students' ability to take on more responsibility for their own learning. In reality, the transition to a self-run classroom can be messy at first, and that is to be expected.

To illustrate the incremental process we undergo in shifting our mindset, let's return for a moment to the language arts teacher who struggled with virtual teaching. When I next visited her online class, I could see evidence of changing priorities and beliefs. Instead of spending class time looking over students' shoulders (virtually, that is) as they wrote their latest story, she began the class with an engaging writing activator. Students were asked to make a list of at least 10 pet peeves, and they wrote with such enthusiasm that when the teacher tried to call everyone together to share, they begged for more time. One girl said, "There are *so* many more than 10 things!" When students began to talk, they could barely be contained. When one boy shared that he cringes when people eat potato chips near him, another boy said, "Hey, I have that too! It's called 'misophonia!'" As more and more students spoke, the teacher sat back and listened. She later told me that she was taking notes on what she heard to help her build stronger relationships, which is the foundation to approaching the second stage of a hands-off teaching style. Most important, when the conversation drew to a natural close, students were in a productive frame of mind. They had spent time writing, thinking, and engaging in discourse. Now, they were ready to work on their stories, and they were also much more receptive to the teacher and to one another.

While the first stage of making change toward hands-off teaching is grounded in mindset, the following chapters move ahead with translating beliefs into action. The truth is, we cannot always wait for mindset shifts to occur; our actions sometimes need to change before our internal beliefs have evolved. In the spirit of a slightly altered catchphrase, "Fake it until you *become* it," teachers can move ahead with hands-off pedagogy even if they have not fully accepted the benefits of the approach. Once they see the change in their students, not to mention in themselves, a true shift in mindset is far more likely to happen as these changes often do: gradually.

Words of Wisdom

In *Never Work Harder Than Your Students and Other Principles of Great Teaching* (2018), author Robyn Jackson shares the importance of allowing students to drive their learning. As part of that process, Jackson discusses the importance of mindset. Some of her most resonant takeaways include:

- While some teachers may be naturally attuned to building classrooms that embrace student agency, most of us need to cultivate the approach more consciously through both mindset and action.
- Typically, teachers work much harder than students to drive the learning, which backfires for both us and our students. Students have less buy-in, and we become frustrated with barriers to progress that we have a difficult time analyzing and removing.
- There is no magic strategy to create a student-centered classroom.

Rather, the overall principles and beliefs that guide our practice make the largest difference in our approach to teaching.

■ The qualities present among master teachers include a constant awareness of where students stand with the learning goal and a focus of quality over quantity, i.e., a "less is more" approach.

Questions for Reflection and Growth

To review the challenges and processes around shifting our mindset away from micromanagement and toward a self-run classroom, consider the following questions both during and after completing the activities in this chapter:

- What is most surprising about the core beliefs that you confronted in your own practice or that a colleague shared?
- When reflecting on your own mindset, what do you see about how you show trust in students and their capacity to drive the learning process? Are there areas that you could improve? What shifts can occur immediately, and what might take more time?
- Which components of the activities for growth provided in this chapter might be useful to share with your colleagues? What is most valuable to you as an individual? What considerations should you bear in mind about implementing these ideas in your own school?
- Think about the stark contrast between helicoptering and hover-free teaching. Is there a middle ground? What might that look like in a classroom?

The Big Idea

The adaptation to a dynamic classroom community cannot move forward without a mindset shift that celebrates the power of student autonomy in learning.

CHAPTER 2

Reframing Relationships: The Second Stage

Jennifer is not a student who typically attracts any special attention from her teachers. Her presence in the classroom is neither note-worthy nor offensive; she sits quietly, does her work as expected, and occasionally ventures a response to a question if the answer is clear-cut. Over the years, teachers have described Jennifer as someone who tries to make herself invisible. Now in seventh grade, Jennifer has begun to draw inward more with each passing month, becoming increasingly hard to verbally engage. She is polite but does not seem interested in class. Despite her gradual withdrawal from class discussions, none of her teachers really seem to notice her growing silence. After all, her grades are good (if not stellar), and there are far more concerning children to help. Jennifer is just fine.

When we encounter a Jennifer, do we ignore her, or do we stop and think about why she might wish to be invisible? The truth is that students like Jennifer slip through the cracks. They are not high achievers or low achievers, and we do not have the time to think about what Jennifer might think of us, or how we might make her class experience a better one. We are too busy giving attention to students who either are already engaged (and are therefore eager to take part in the class) or who show their lack of engagement unproductively by acting out. However, if we were to really stop and think about all the students who hide in the periphery of our classes, the ones who look at us a lot but say very little, we might unlock the door to building the kinds of relationships that really matter in teaching. We could focus on providing students with a safe environment in which academic risk-taking is encouraged, wrong answers are celebrated, and all students are able to learn on their own terms.

How are students gradually shut down, and what can we do to stop it? So much of our messaging as teachers is unintentional, but increasing our awareness of how students see our classes is the first step to creating a space that fosters deeper relationships. Suppose we follow Jennifer into her seventh-grade Life Science class. On this day, the class is learning about symbiotic relationships. At the front of the room, the teacher shares the definitions of three kinds of symbiosis: mutualism, commensalism, and parasitism. She turns to the class. "Who can share an example of parasitism with us?"

Jennifer hesitates. She thinks she knows what a parasite is. After all, she had lice a few years ago, and her mom explained that as Jennifer scratched madly at her head, the lice were benefiting from the blood in her scalp. Against the voice in her head telling her to stay quiet, Jennifer raises her hand. The teacher, unused to seeing Jennifer's hand and wishing to encourage her, calls on her right away. "Yes, Jennifer?"

Jennifer is nervous and forgets all about the lice as she struggles to remember what she was about to say. On the wall, there is a poster with a lion on it. Ashamed to admit that she forgot her answer, Jennifer grasps at a perceived lifeline. "It's like when a lion eats a mouse. The mouse dies, but the lion benefits."

At this point, the teacher at the front of the room has a split-second decision to make. Jennifer's answer is not technically correct, as the lion is a predator, not a parasite. Suppose that the teacher responds honestly to Jennifer and says, "You are close, but that's not quite right. Who has another example? John?"

In this first version of the scenario, the teacher certainly intends to encourage Jennifer by telling her that the answer is in the right neighborhood, even though it is technically wrong. In other words, the teacher's intentions are good, and she probably does not realize the effect her response may have on Jennifer and on their relationship moving forward. After all, Jennifer is polite and quiet, and the teacher has no visible evidence that Jennifer is doubting herself. In Jennifer's head, however, a very different scene is playing out. She sits in her seat, feeling embarrassed and ashamed, not to mention angry at both herself and the teacher. She took a risk, she panicked, and she was wrong. She hates this class. The teacher does not like her anyway, and she plays favorites. Jennifer will never talk in class again, ever.

As teachers, it is impossible for us to read minds. We have no idea what students really think of us, and it's challenging to make their perspective more transparent. Jennifer's science teacher means to be helpful and she cannot see that Jennifer has internally reacted to this short exchange in such a dramatic way. As a seventh grader, Jennifer cares deeply about how others perceive her, and this brief moment has been blown up in her mind to be incredibly significant. She no longer trusts herself to make valuable contributions in class, and she trusts the teacher even less. The future of their relationship is in extreme jeopardy, though only Jennifer knows it.

We may not be able to intuit what students are thinking, but we can use the information we have to increase our awareness and prevent incidents like the one above from occurring. For example, middle schoolers care deeply about how others see them, perhaps more so than children who are slightly younger or older. Even seemingly insignificant conversations or exchanges can be magnified in their view. As school counselor and licensed therapist Phyllis Fagell writes, "For middle-schoolers, even minor incidents can be distressing" (2019). We know from our teaching experience that while raising a hand in class to share a reply might be easy for some students, it represents a significant social and academic risk for others. If a child who is typically quieter decides to speak out, we may wish to proceed more carefully than we would with a child whose hand is constantly shooting into the air.

With the idea in mind of reaching a more reluctant student, let's consider a slightly different outcome to the same scenario. In this other version, the teacher has asked the same question about examples of symbiosis. Jennifer has thought about her lice experience, raised her hand, forgotten her response, and improvised with the lion and mouse. As the teacher listens to Jennifer, her heart sinks a little. She knows that Jennifer is hesitant to speak up and wants to make sure that she validates whatever response she hears, even this incorrect one. In this teacher's classroom, all answers are celebrated, even—or especially—the wrong ones. The teacher has to pick her next words very carefully.

She begins with a positive focus on what Jennifer did well: "I really appreciate how you picked an example that harms one animal while helping the other. Tell me a little more, Jennifer. How is the lion benefiting? Can you elaborate with some detail?"

Inwardly, Jennifer relaxes a little. The teacher is not shutting her down or calling on another student. She is asking her to talk more about her ideas. "Well," Jennifer says, "the lion is eating the mouse, so I guess that means he gets the benefit of being fed." As she talks, she is aware of hands shooting up all around her, and a boy in the corner is shaking his head. Jennifer begins to feel nervous all over again, but the teacher does not look at the other students. She remains focused on Jennifer.

"Okay," says the teacher. "Now, Jennifer, let's look at our definition on the board of parasitism. What kinds of benefits do parasites get from their hosts?"

At this moment, the teacher is redirecting Jennifer. She knows that Jennifer is most likely able to figure out how to answer the question correctly and she will stick with her until that happens. However, the lion example is a nonstarter, so the teacher has opted to circle back to the symbiosis definitions to help Jennifer regroup. Instead of calling on the other students who are trying to share their own answers, the teacher chooses to work with the student who decided to take a risk and raise her hand, the one who is typically so reserved.

As Jennifer looks at the definition again, she remembers the lice. "Oh!" she says, suddenly excited. "Parasites depend on the host for the benefit of survival. They live on the surface of the host, or even inside. So the lion thing doesn't work, but head lice is a good example of parasitism, right?" Her relief is palpable.

The teacher nods. "That is exactly right, Jennifer. How many of you have had lice?" Several hands go up, this time in a positive response to what Jennifer has shared. "Class, Jennifer brings up an illustration that so many of you have experienced." As the teacher goes on to explain how lice benefit from animal hosts and the class veers into a slight tangent about another student's horrific experience with a particularly nasty case of superlice, Jennifer begins to smile. She did not just think of a correct example; she thought of one that everyone understands. Her initial response about the lion still hurts a little, but she can brush it aside because she knows the teacher believed in her, trusted her to find her way to the right answer, and will continue to validate her contributions to the class.

Even if Jennifer had not recalled her lice example at that moment, her ideas have been given value. Suppose that Jennifer cannot find the correct answer in that moment of increased pressure. The teacher is still able to skillfully take any potentially negative focus off Jennifer by directing the class to turn and talk about parasitic relationships, or to move on in a similar way that is not embarrassing to Jennifer.

The specific takeaways to remember when calling on students or singling them out in any way are:

- Validate all answers, correct or otherwise, by using them to move the entire class understanding of a concept forward.
- Do not call on other students to provide the "right" or desired answer, as this practice is an unspoken way of removing confidence from the student who responded first.
- Stop and make instruction clear if a student shows confusion. If one student is confused, it is likely that other students are in the same boat.

Even when situations are not resolved as smoothly as Jennifer's, the takeaways above will ensure that students understand that the classroom is a safe space for answering questions, sharing ideas, and putting themselves forward. For example, had Jennifer never remembered her lice example, the teacher could backtrack to the posted definitions, provide some clarity, and ask students to demonstrate their understanding of what the definitions mean before moving ahead. That would remove any negative spotlight from Jennifer and place the responsibility for learning back on the class as a whole.

Teaching is a series of quick decisions, and while we sometimes make the wrong ones, we can learn and do better next time. So much of the relationship-building we do as teachers is unspoken, so thinking about the intention behind how we build relationships increases the likelihood that we will pause before making any missteps. If students see our efforts and know we trust them, they are more apt to engage with their learning and take ownership of what they do, solidifying their investment in our classes. When we keep relationship-building on a surface level, we send the implicit message that we care about our students only as people and not necessarily as learners. However, when we extend those relationships by making them relevant to the instructional realm, we build connections that transcend good rapport and encourage a higher level of achievement, student agency, and mutual respect.

As we discovered in Chapter 1 with the first stage of a hands-off classroom, moving away from micromanaging habits and embracing a more flexible mindset is a vital first step in the journey to achieving a classroom that celebrates the power of student autonomy. While creating more awareness around our mindset is where we begin to explore a teaching model that serves students with more agility, we cannot truly step back and share ownership of our classes unless there is a sense of mutual trust between our students and ourselves. Building that trust begins with both examining how meaningful relationships function and going beyond simply establishing good personal rapport with students. If our purpose is that students feel comfortable enough in our classes to take academic risks and feel a shared sense of responsibility for their success, we need to extend our relationship-building practices to instruction. That goal can be achieved when we build our capacity around creating deeper connections with students—that is, once we have an awareness of what to look for. In order to do that, we must explore how we have typically built relationships in the past, what we can do to adjust our methods to empower student learning, and why trust that is explicitly connected to academic experience is so vitally important.

Trust Before Teaching

One of my colleagues used to talk about a teacher he really loved in high school, someone he admired greatly and hoped to emulate. He did not really focus on what happened in the classroom; his fond memories stemmed from the fact that this teacher would play football with his male students during break times. When I asked him more targeted questions about the teacher's practice inside the classroom, or what my friend learned that stayed with him all these years later, he shared his recollection that the teacher was somewhat haphazard in how he conducted his class. Rather than structuring lessons around assessments or class assignments, for example, much of the content was covered in a continual back-and-forth conversation between the teacher and his most vocal students.

As we talked more about this teacher and his methods, I began to wonder about the experience of students in the class who did not meet certain criteria. What about the female students, who were not invited to play football? What about the male students who did not enjoy playing football? And in the classroom itself, how did the students who did not have this opportunity to bond with the teacher during their free time feel about his treatment of those who did? Was there bias toward the football players, either real or perceived? And if the conversations about class content were not grounded in any specific structures, did the students who did not personally connect with this teacher feel comfortable making contributions in his class?

More often than not, the idea of building relationships is seen as a personal endeavor, and the teachers who are perceived as "cool" or popular might spend a lot of time and energy connecting with students either outside of the classroom or during noninstructional time in the classroom. While teachers of this description are typically well liked and intend to be inclusive, they may unwittingly create divisions among students that lead to undesired results. For example, many of us have sat in classrooms with teachers who have stellar reputations. As students, we enter these classrooms with high expectations. What happens, then, if the teacher bonds only with certain students, has a sense of humor that is not universal, or has interests that are not inclusive? Granted, we can only please some of the people some of the time, and we should not set an unattainable standard of perfection for our teaching. However, in sharing pieces of ourselves when we bond with students, do we take time to make sure that we are reaching out to everyone in the room and not just the people we naturally gravitate toward?

The process of checking our own methods for connecting with students is grounded in the awareness we have about how we build trust.

As teachers, we often dedicate particular times within a class period to building rapport. For example, we tend to use both the minutes before instruction begins and the time spent packing up toward the end to socialize with our students. Many teachers also spend the first 10 minutes or so of each class doing a warm-up that is engaging and sets the tone for the remainder of the class period. The question is, are these efforts enough to facilitate a strong sense of self-efficacy and confidence in students to the point that they want to share ownership of the learning by making frequent contributions and also feel comfortable doing so?

Unfortunately, the answer to the question above is no. As teachers, we sometimes forget the significant influence we have over our students. They may admire us or fear us, but neither of those reactions is what we are aiming for. Instead, we want them to feel comfortable collaborating with us. It is always nice when we can find common ground with our students. For example, earlier in my career, I shared a love of baking all things peanut butter and chocolate with one of my 11th graders and we would swap recipes with abandon. However, that does not mean that she trusted me to support her in what we learned during instructional time, or that other students in the class did not feel left out of the peripheral connection that baking brought to our relationship. Looking back, I cannot say with any certainty that this student shared her learning of writing skills as freely as she shared her culinary skills, and I made the classic mistake of thinking that our teacher-student relationship was effective when really, it was our person-to-person relationship that was more functional. Furthermore, I never stopped to wonder whether other students saw this connection and felt bad because they were not part of it. And most important of all, I did not build the trust needed to make sure that this student, as well as all of my students, had the agency needed to push the learning beyond what was comfortable.

Until we have taught students that they can trust us to support their learning and that we are their advocates, they will not be able to own any part of our classes, and we will not be able to stop micromanaging them. Therefore, reframing our relationships strategically is an indispensable part of moving toward a more hands-off classroom model. With just a few adjustments to our methods, not to mention some instructional strategies that help us make the transition to a safer and more open learning space for students, we can move one step closer to stepping back and ensuring that learning is a collaborative experience.

Strategies for Building Deeper Relationships

Targeting deeper relationship-building in our lesson planning should have a strong tie-in to what we want students to achieve. We run into difficulty when we do not make a clear connection between how teachers and students interact with each other and the way that relationships play into the establishment of a safe learning space. We are very aware of the need to make students comfortable in class, particularly at the start of an instructional period, but sometimes that priority does not bear out for the remainder of the class.

As an illustration, during a visit to a middle school social studies department meeting, I was asked to weigh in on how the teachers were developing connections with students. The teachers, all sitting in a circle, shared some beautifully creative ideas with one another. For example, one teacher played a game in which students needed to agree on a common definition of soup. If any liquid food in a bowl was defined as soup, did chocolate sauce count? Or if the food was defined by certain other parameters (e.g., could be eaten with a spoon), was cereal really soup? Was temperature significant? The teacher shared the enthusiasm of her students for this conversation and how lively the debate became as the class worked toward a shared understanding.

After the meeting, I met with the department chair to debrief. To begin, we agreed that the teachers were dedicated to creating a safe learning space for their students and that they had excellent ideas in terms of how to achieve this goal. We also agreed that while the opening activities were a lot of fun, they did not necessarily connect to the lesson that followed. For example, I asked if the teacher doing the community builder on soup was teaching a unit focused on debate, because the activity could be an excellent way to prepare students to structure logical arguments, and the answer was no. More often than not, these opening warm-ups teachers shared existed for the primary purpose of bringing students into the class period in a welcoming and enjoyable way. While getting students off to a good start is a worthy purpose and does help with building trust, does it accomplish the entire goal of building a relationship that continues to be meaningful once the learning has begun?

The problem with keeping a sense of rapport or connection separate from academic content is that students make a distinction in their minds between a teacher's personal interest in them and the teacher's belief that they can learn. They might think something like, "Mr. Jones likes me, but he knows I'm not good at math." Aside from the obvious issue with any student feeling this way, these thoughts are usually hidden from the teacher, who thinks all is well. That is why we might think our students really like us or enjoy our classes, but when we give student-voice surveys and they respond anonymously, their perceptions can sometimes emerge as startlingly unfavorable comments.

How do we break this cycle of misunderstanding and ensure that when we build trust in our classrooms, it goes beyond the surface level? How do we know for sure, both in what we observe and in what students share, that they know we believe in them as people and as learners? Figure 2.1 shares three examples of classroom strategies that not only increase positive interactions between teachers and students but also have the potential to connect to instructional goals, depending on the lessons or themes being presented in a unit of study.

To accommodate more than one possible learning setting while injecting some flexibility into the strategies, each activity contains a "virtual twist" for students who may not be in physical proximity to one another. Whether that adjustment is necessary or not, the three strategies above all have one thing in common: They send a clear message that all contributions to class are legitimate and will be celebrated, and as a result, the strategies help to build each student's trust in the teacher's intentions.

When we work on implementing the second stage of hands-off teaching by building trusting relationships that promote academic rigor and risk-taking, we do not have to reinvent our methods from the ground up. Instead, we can think about how some of our most tried-and-true activators both align with the content we teach and promote strong relationships. Figure 2.2 contains a list of possible activity ideas that allow us to accomplish the joint goal of fostering meaningful connections with students while incorporating what we teach as it fits.

FIGURE 2.1   STRATEGIES FOR BUILDING DEEPER RELATIONSHIPS

STRATEGY

My Favorite Mistake

DESCRIPTION

This strategy works particularly well in math and science courses, but it can be used in any situation where answers to a question might be more concrete. The teacher asks a question and students, often anonymously, write a response on a slip of paper. The teacher collects the papers and shares the answers. Once everyone has heard the responses, the teacher picks a "favorite mistake," which is an incorrect answer that is most helpful in uncovering common errors or misconceptions.

Virtual Twist: Instead of using slips of paper, students can share their answers on a shared online document or in an online meeting chat box.

PURPOSE

By purposely celebrating answers that are incorrect, the teacher facilitates a safe learning space where all student contributions have value. Furthermore, this activity focuses on the standard for success and not on individual students, which contributes to a sense of common purpose in meeting the learning goal.

STRATEGY

Past Me, Present Me

DESCRIPTION

Near the end of class, students are instructed to take a sheet of paper and fold it in half (both horizontal and vertical folds work). On one side, they write down a perception they had about the day's learning before instruction, which represents "Past Me." On the other side, they write down what they now understand or know, which represents "Present Me."

Virtual Twist: Use an online tool such as a Jamboard (a mechanism for attaching sticky notes to different web boards; see note below the chart) to get a clearly visible collection of student responses. Students can post their "Past Me" and "Present Me" ideas under the specified page headings.

PURPOSE

This activity emphasizes the power of self-examination and legitimizes the growth-mindset idea that while we might not know everything, we get smarter each day. By making it clear that nobody is expected to know it all, the classroom becomes a more comfortable arena for academic risk-taking. Furthermore, this activity makes the value of daily learning transparent and clear to students as they identify small changes or developments in their acquisition of smaller daily objectives.

STRATEGY

One Word

DESCRIPTION

After learning a new concept or skill, students are given Post-it Notes and put into small groups (i.e., pairs or groups of three). Each student is instructed to write just one word on the Post-it that summarizes the most important part of what they have just learned. In their groups, students look at one another's Post-its and try to guess what larger idea that word represents. When the groups are done, all students in the class are directed to put their Post-its on the walls, walk around, and either check off the ones they most understand or agree with, or put a question mark on ones they would like to discuss further.

Virtual Twist: This same exercise can be replicated in virtual breakout rooms, with the final one-word responses going onto a Padlet (see note below the chart) or similar tool.

PURPOSE

When students work in small groups to bounce ideas off one another and refine their responses, they are less likely to feel as though their answers are a trap or a "gotcha." As a result, they learn to trust one another and the teacher more. Furthermore, sharing ideas with a smaller group before sharing with the entire class, and doing so in a less verbal way, accommodates multiple learning styles and gives all students a voice, which is another strong trust-building strategy.

Note: Virtual tools are explained in further depth at the close of this chapter.

FIGURE 2.2   FLEXIBLE ACTIVATOR IDEAS

DETAILS DUMP

Before teaching new content, put students into teams. Each team is given broad-strokes information about what the new learning is (ie., topic, possible themes, etc.). In their teams, students must write down as many details or pieces of information about the content as they can collectively brainstorm within a specific timeframe When finished, each group posts its results. The team that "wins" has the highest number of accurate details. After the activity ends, the teacher can use what students already know to inform and tailor instruction.

TWEET IT!

Using the Twitter 280-character limit, ask students to "tweet" a summarizer of the day's lesson on a shared class document or board. These tweets can be discussed at the close of class or the opening of the following day's learning, and the teacher can also use the tweets to check for understanding.

LOVE, LOVE NOT

Ask students to share one element of the previous day's lesson they enjoyed or benefited from and one they felt was not as helpful. This quick feedback method allows for more targeted planning as units proceed and also helps us gain a deeper understanding of how our students prefer to learn.

A PICTURE IS WORTH . . .

Display an image that somehow connects to the learning goal. Ask students to brainstorm a question or comment about how the image might relate to the topic or content at hand. Students can share their contributions any number of ways, and their responses will help guide the teacher to next steps.

20 QUESTIONS

To modify the popular road-trip game, one student thinks of a course-related topic or idea while the class takes turns asking 20 questions to determine the answer. After a few rounds, students are usually in a more engaged mindset for active learning.

WHAT IF?

Ask students to brainstorm a "What if?" question about course content. In history, it might be a change in an event. In English, it might be about a literary plot. In math, it could be a different pathway to solving a problem. Once students share their questions, the class can work on answering the "what if" scenarios in a variety of ways, either in groups or individually.

ONE THING

Ask students to think about the "it" of the day's lesson, or the one most important idea they will take away. Students can record this in any number of places. It is the teacher's decision to share out in that moment, or to use the responses in an activator the following class period.

All of the activities in Figure 2.2 share some commonalities. The provided options work in multiple content areas, in multiple ways. They can be adapted to suit teacher or student preference, not to mention be conducted pretty much anywhere, from remote locations to a physical classroom space. These activities also help to build meaningful academic interactions and allow relationships to grow not just consistently but in conjunction with curriculum goals. Essentially, when we build activities that are both engaging and relevant (such as the examples in Figures 2.1 and 2.2) into our instruction, we communicate a belief that we not only like the students in front of us but also believe in them—and that is far more powerful.

How to Reframe Relationships: Do This, Not That

Reframing the ways in which we build trust with students does not have to be any kind of seismic shift. Rather, small changes can make an even bigger impact on how students feel about their learning environment. The chart below (Figure 2.3) shares examples of more traditional instructional practices (i.e., the "Before") and then suggests strategic upgrades (i.e., the "After") to include a stronger link between extending trust and instruction.

The two columns in Figure 2.3 point to how we have historically approached instruction in a more traditional model versus how the process of relationship-building for mutual trust can be incorporated into standard teaching and learning processes. Note that many of these "After" upgrades speak to increased student choice and voice. In a classroom that allows the teacher to step back and share ownership, students must feel safe expressing how they wish to learn, and we must be flexible and open-minded enough to consider their input.

While classrooms that are not overly controlled may appear effortless to an outside observer, a lot of work and planning goes into how a teacher intentionally implements routines and structures to create the appropriate space for removing the need to helicopter over students. While building relationships opens the door to a safe environment, the next step to achieving a hands-off classroom is grounded in how we prepare to engage students. Think back to Jennifer and her experience in seventh-grade science class; the second scenario is an illustration of how a trusting

FIGURE 2.3 BEFORE VERSUS AFTER: REFRAMING RELATIONSHIP-BUILDING

BEFORE	AFTER
Greet students at the door with a smile and a high five, quick conversation, or other brief interchange.	Greet students at the door with a smile and a quick hello or bit of small talk, then hand them a slip of paper (to be discussed in a few minutes, allowing for processing time) with an accessible, open-ended question or comment related to the learning from the previous day.
Do a fun warm-up.	Activate learning with an engaging activity that stimulates thinking and connects to the daily content objective.
Assess student mastery primarily with worksheets, quizzes, or other traditional handouts.	In addition to using more traditional methods of assessment, gauge student mastery with opportunities for discourse (such as a Socratic seminar or group conversation), small projects, or self-selected choices such as short videos or journal entries.
Plan every lesson without student input.	On a regular basis, check in with students about how they are doing by collecting feedback (survey, form, etc.) that directs possible next steps; be sure to always point out when making an instructional change as a response to feedback.
Grade student work and provide only a letter or number grade, without any other information.	When assigning work, put a clear list of expected criteria in student-friendly language onto the assignment and discuss expectations, solicit questions, and clear up confusion; then, attach the same criteria to the graded assignment and check off what the student met and did not meet (yet), to provide added clarity.
Center instruction mainly around teacher talk or direct instruction.	Provide students with ample opportunities to demonstrate their learning in a variety of ways to match learning styles or preferences.

relationship leads to heightened engagement. Now that Jennifer knows that her teacher will stick with her and support her, she is far more likely to approach her learning with enthusiasm, with added confidence, and with the belief that she has important contributions to make to the class.

Words of Wisdom

In "Never Say Anything a Kid Can Say!" (2000), author and teacher Steven Reinhart shares the importance of talking less so that students can share their learning more and so that our relationships reflect a mutual trust that ties directly to instruction. Through an appealing use of anecdote, he explains strategies that detail how we ask questions to enhance student confidence around their academic identities. Some of Reinhart's suggestions are:

- Ask higher-order thinking questions that are open ended and promote critical-thinking skills to show students our belief in their academic capabilities.
- Instead of repeating students' answers in our own words, which can seem as though we might be trying to improve upon what they have said, employ wait time to see if the student elaborates. Also, give other students time to add their thoughts to the conversation.
- Find low-risk ways to solicit several answers to the same question so that multiple students have opportunities to share how they understand the learning.
- If students show confusion when asked a question, give them a chance to work together in small groups before responding in front of the larger group.
- When students express confusion about class content, encourage them to phrase their feelings as a specific question rather than a general "I don't understand."

Questions for Reflection and Growth

Before moving to the third stage of a hands-off classroom, which centers on student engagement and investment, think about the most valuable takeaways from this chapter and how that learning might translate into next steps. Use these questions to guide your thought process:

- When you were a student, did you have teachers who created a safe learning space in which you felt valued? If not, how did that feel? How did your experiences as a student influence your current identity and practices as a teacher?
- What is one realization you had as you read this chapter? Why is it significant?
- Think about the strategies and ideas shared in this chapter. Which one would you like to try first, and how will you adapt it to fit your teaching style?
- Think of one way you build relationships that makes you proud. If the technique you are thinking of addresses more personal than academic needs, how can you ground that practice more firmly in instruction?

The Big Idea

Without mutual trust, teachers cannot step back and share classroom ownership with students. We build that trust during instruction by encouraging academic risk-taking in a safe learning space.

Virtual Tools Referenced in Chapter 2

- Jamboard: This interactive tool functions as an online board. Teachers are able to post questions or tasks on the Jamboard, which contains multiple pages that are easy to move through with arrows. Students can create virtual sticky notes and post them on numbered pages. Everyone on the Jamboard collaborates and sees responses in real time. Jamboard has a number of other functions as well, including the ability to create or share images.
- Padlet: This tool functions as an online board that allows both students and teachers to post ideas onto a common page in a number of different configurations. If the teacher allows the class, students can also comment upon one another's posts.

CHAPTER 3

From Engagement to Investment: The Third Stage

We hold great influence over the students in front of us, and we can use that power in any number of ways. If our aim (conscious or not) is to reproduce learners just like us, our strategies will backfire; when we use our own academic experiences to shape how we design instruction for others, we fail to engage a fairly wide swath of the students in our classes. If we instead allow students to build their own image of who they want to be as learners, we can simultaneously empower students and help them achieve their goals. The key to avoiding the first approach lies in how we draw students into the role of shaping relevant learning experiences.

Empowering All Learners

A few years ago, after a 10-year break from teaching ninth grade, I once again entered the world of freshman English. Having spent the intervening years teaching both Advanced Placement and creative writing courses to upperclassmen, being with younger students once more was quite a jolt back into reality. Over the past 10 years, I had forgotten a lot of what I knew about creating structures for intrinsic motivation in the face of working with more mature students. Suddenly, I had a room full of energetic 14-year-olds, many of whom were both easily distracted and desirous of wandering around the classroom rather than sitting down. While the barriers I encountered with engaging my students might have looked at first glance like a classroom management issue, I quickly realized that flaws in my instructional approach were far more significant than any kind of behavior techniques I had in my repertoire.

Early in the year, it became clear that a boy who sat near the front was going to present a particular challenge. He was usually very friendly, though his main goal was to distract me during class so that our conversations could become more personal and highly tangential rather than focused on the lesson. When thwarted, however, this student became withdrawn or sulky, turning his desk toward the wall and refusing to do any of the work. I tried any number of strategies to help him engage, but most of them focused on his external behavior rather than the root cause of his actions. For example, I let him use a "fidget" to keep his hands busy, and I made sure to check in on him both before and after class each day. After several weeks of experimenting with different tactics and not seeing any improvement, I finally made some headway one day, and quite by accident.

The class was in the middle of working with interpreting informational texts and the article we were reading happened to be about the steps needed to become a licensed driver. The class cross-referenced the article with a state webpage on laws for getting a permit and a license, just to make the article a little more relatable for students on the cusp of their education as drivers. Throughout the class period, the boy in front sat up straighter, underlined the vocabulary words he was asked to annotate, scribbled questions in the margins, and kept flipping back and forth through the pages of the article, drinking them in again and again. His focus on the text was completely different than it had been with any other piece of reading we had encountered that year. During our discussion of the article, he shared well-considered ideas that were on point, and he did so courteously. At the end of class, I walked over to him. "You did such good work today," I said. "You really stepped up."

"Well, yeah," he said, as though it were the most obvious thing in the world. "Today's reading was interesting."

"It's not interesting on other days?"

The boy pulled the article out of his backpack. "See this?" he asked, pointing to the rapidly crumpling pages. "I really love cars and I can't wait to be old enough to drive, but nobody ever told me about how that works. Like, I don't know the rules in our state for when I can get my permit, or even what I need to do. This doesn't have everything I need to know, but at least it helped a little."

"Okay," I said, "but not everything we read in class is about something in real life. Some of it is made up, like fiction. Are you interested in that?"

The boy thought about it for a minute. "Not really," he admitted. "I'm interested in what I want to do, like drive. Or carpentry. I'm going into a career-prep program for that, and I want to learn more about it."

As we continued the conversation, I began thinking about how to balance my student's engagement with nonfiction texts that applied to his interests with the very real need to teach him about interpreting other kinds of reading as well. In the end, we struck a deal of sorts: As much as possible with any text we studied, he could self-select either from an array I presented or from the library, but the reading had to match the genre of the text the entire class studied. He also understood that sometimes I could not give him that choice, particularly during assessments or in times when the class needed to study a common theme or time period. Furthermore, he would need to take a more active and productive role in keeping me informed about his feelings with the course materials and not channel his frustration into inappropriate behavior.

It would be stretching the truth to say that we never had any difficulty with each other again. There were days when he expressed his disengagement in disruptive ways, and there were days when I did not give him choices that matched his interests. However, we both made more of an effort to understand each other, and we also kept our lines of communication open. Over the course of the next several months, I saw a marked improvement in this student's reading skills, in his intrinsic motivation, and in his desire to make an effective effort to reach academic goals. As a result, his growth was visible, both to me and to those around him. In addition, his classmates benefited from the same flexibility that I began to provide to everyone: choosing their own texts where appropriate and having a stronger voice in how we learned. As the students became more invested in their active learning roles, I was able to give them more free-dom to make even more choices regarding how they moved forward, and I no longer had to place myself in constant physical proximity to students and hover over them in order to make sure they were focused. In other words, class was a shared responsibility, everyone was more engaged, and we were all a whole lot happier.

Winning Them Over

While the second stage of building a hands-off classroom (i.e., integrating relationships into instructional content and building a classroom environ-ment of trust) is a vital step in the process, we know too well that even when we do everything we should be doing, some students will still not engage with our lessons. With this challenge in mind, we must not only establish meaningful relationships and assume that engagement with learning will take care of itself; we must also make a concentrated effort to keep working on our connections with students so that we can more effectively engage them cognitively in the learning. The best way to win people over is to understand them; when we have specific methods for uncovering how students want to learn, we can apply strategies from our repertoire that optimize the cognitive process and empower students to learn without our constant oversight.

It is one thing to say that we must prioritize student independence to foster true engagement, but quite another to make that happen. How do we actualize the goal of placing engagement on our "must do" list in alignment with curriculum design and lesson planning and before we move ahead to instruction? The answer lies both in how we look at stu-dent motivation and in how we let our views guide us in making sure our classes are as relevant as possible to student experiences. When we rely on externally motivating factors to engage students, such as grades, any buy-in we get is a result of students' surface-level desire to achieve in a particular teacher's class.

However, a successful grade does not mean that students care about what they learn, and it also does not account for the many preteens and teens who are not motivated by external factors. As writer Tara Garcia Mathewson points out:

In many schools, students do their work because their teachers tell them to. Or because they need to do it to get a certain grade. . . . For other students, they need minimum grades to be on sports teams or participate in extracurricular activities or please their parents, and that becomes their motivation. Students who do their work because they're genuinely interested in learning the material are few and far between. (Mathewson, 2019, para. 4)

External motivation is finicky and unstable, depending on each student's "why" for compliance with a grading system. For example, an actor who needs good grades to be eligible to perform in the school play may disengage once that motivator no longer exists. Therefore, our goal should be to tap into the intrinsic desire to learn for every student in order to produce both authentic and long-lasting results so that the "few and far between" students Mathewson references become the many.

What is the best way to flip our approach so that instead of pushing students to complete tasks by rewarding or punishing them (i.e., extrinsic methods for motivation), we create a space where they are eager and inwardly driven to take an active role in the class? The answer lies in how we plan our classes intentionally for peak relevance and engagement. By thinking about how we approach the learning not solely from a completion-of-curriculum standpoint but more from the perspective of how students will react to the lessons, we can be far more successful in our efforts to engage the class. For example, if I know that in the following week I will be teaching a lesson on developing a research question, I can ask students for some playful topics to practice with ahead of time and then incorporate their ideas into my planning. Or, if we have a long-term project coming up, I might think about the rationale behind what we're doing a little more carefully. Do I want students to learn about a specific topic, or do I want them to learn more general skills, such as creating a slideshow presentation?

If the former, my job is to make the assigned topic as accessible as possible to students with varied learning styles. If the latter, I have more leeway in how I engage each student in learning about the presentation process, in that the criteria for success can be geared toward a skill rather than a topic. A student who is passionate about video games might be eager to exhaustively look into the history of the gaming industry, or a student who loves baseball might want to read about the game-changing theory behind *Moneyball* by Michael Lewis. Either way, our focus is on helping students build skills that apply beyond our classes, not simply driving content for its own sake. When we plan our classes with the lens of students as lifelong learners in mind, having a flexible mindset and a heightened awareness of our goals helps us determine what parts of the assignment are nonnegotiable and what parts can be adjusted to be more appealing to students.

It should also be noted that when we plan for engagement, we consider a variety of situations and settings as part of that process. That way, the process of reaching students relies less on where we are and more on what we do. The tools in this chapter apply to both proximal and remote school settings. Once we get more comfortable with a more dynamic model of planning, one that shifts with agility in response to the conditions around us, we can truly accomplish the third stage of increasing not just students' engagement but also their investment in our class community. That accomplishment puts us one step closer to achieving a classroom that is not micromanaged by one but rather shared by all.

Planning for Engagement

Is it possible for an educational approach to serve everyone nearly all the time? From a deficit mindset, the idea of reaching all students sounds like a fantasy, but the purpose of achieving a classroom free of micromanagement is to empower students in ways that cannot be accomplished under a more static construct. Think about the challenge of tailoring instruction to students when they are taught in the more traditional model of desks in rows, in one location only. It is impossible for us to be everywhere at once, and this reality is no more apparent than when students learn a new concept and we are flitting around the classroom, trying to help multiple students at once as hands go higher in the air and some students appear to levitate off their seats in their anxiety to be assisted. Unless we have significant adult support in the room (and let's face it, most of us do not), the idea of helping children reach individualized goals becomes impossible.

Insanity is often jokingly defined as doing the same thing repeatedly and expecting different results. We laugh when we hear this, but in education, our status quo systems keep us in the same frustrating place that produces mediocre (or worse) results more often than not. If we want to move past minimum competency when it comes to serving all students, our approach to responding to needs that change as quickly as our students grow has to be grounded in strategies that support constant shifts in practice. When we create classrooms that take each individual student into account while still serving the whole group, we are able to slowly build the autonomy of students both in and out of class, which consequently provides us with more time to watch students, listen to them, and figure out what each learner needs.

The evolution of our role from sole directors to collaborative designers of learning is central to creating an environment with time to focus on individual students. Picture a traditional classroom in which students are given independent work time to complete a presentation. In a standard setup, all of the students in class are expected to work on the same stages of the presentation at the same time, regardless of where they might be in the process. For example, if the presentation outline is due on Tuesday, students might be asked to complete their drafts Monday and meet with the teacher for in-class conferences on Tuesday. As well intentioned as we are in hoping that the class reaches learning goals as a group, the expectation that all students are in the same place at the same time is more aspirational than realistic. Furthermore, it is not wise to hope that effective individual conferences with every member of the class can logistically take place before a static due date, even if we rush through them. If we really think about it, the time factor of when assignments are handed in may not be especially important. Perhaps we have been conditioned to hold students to so-called real-world deadlines when they are not yet in a situation that requires such firm compliance. Even adults who are in the "real world" do not usually show such rigidity with timelines, so why should students be held to strict time constraints when it comes to completing work, when a deadline often occurs at the expense of real growth? Isn't mastery of learning more important than a date that is often arbitrary?

Adjusting our classroom approach to focus on overarching goals with flexible means of achieving outcomes may include more forethought in the planning stages of teaching, but it frees up our time during class so that more engaging instruction is possible. Picture that same class that needs to complete a presentation by a certain due date. What if we provided a more fluid set of expectations for the stages that are needed to complete the presentation? Suppose that the presentation outline, due on Tuesday in the previous classroom scenario, were due with a goal date of Tuesday but with an option for submitting later in the week with the proviso of a required conversation between the teacher and student about what is happening? While we might be concerned that there is not enough time to meet with students who are behind, Figure 3.1 demonstrates how a lesson plan might proactively address the needs of each student. We can use this template to plan lessons over the course of one or more class periods. Unlike a typical lesson-planning tool, which often relies on a calendar, this one contains a series of open-ended questions that spur our thinking about the important factors of a successful lesson, from big-picture considerations such as learning outcomes to smaller but equally vital processes around student choice and response.

Teachers who are intentional with advance planning for engagement create an environment in which students participate actively in learning. Furthermore, though no dates are indicated yet, planning tools like the one shown in Figure 3.1 actually help us gain time that we really need to assist individual students during class. As an added bonus, when we plan for engagement and focus on meeting the learning goal with the consideration of intrinsic motivation at the fore, any final products that students submit are no longer a mystery to us in terms of what we will be grading. The simple act of being more familiar with expectations and processes as an assignment is completed gradually in manageable chunks and shared with the teacher places less pressure on students to demystify how well they might meet expectations. It also results in less anxiety on our part about having to provide quality feedback to our students within an acceptable period of time since we have seen the projects develop, are more familiar with what the final products will look like, and can therefore more promptly provide students with feedback on a clear set of criteria for success.

As always, when we plan lessons, we should not work in a bubble. It is standard to collaborate with our colleagues, but how often do we

FIGURE 3.1   DYNAMIC PLANNING GUIDE

What is the desired learning outcome? What are the main expectations of this assignment?	Example: *Students will be able to identify the rules of soccer.*
What teacher-directed elements are needed for students to meet the expectations?	Example: *I need to create a clear handout with all of the rules explained.*
What can students accomplish without help?	Example: *Students can talk to one another about the rules they already understand.*
How can students exercise choice throughout this process, both with the work itself and with deadlines?	Example: *I have a video, a slideshow, and the handout students can access to understand the rules better. They will be showing their understanding through playing the game, so those who feel ready can practice on their own or with a partner.*
What materials are needed for students to be both autonomous and successful?	Example: *In addition to the resources above, I need soccer balls, cones, and the net set up.*
How will I determine whether students have met the learning goal?	Example: *Students will complete an exit ticket that explains the rules.*
If students need more time to reach the outcomes, what are some conferencing questions to ask when discussing individual needs?	*Example: Would it help for me to show you an example? To demonstrate with the soccer ball?*

factor students into the lesson-planning process? In the spirit of "help me help you," it is more than a little strange that our traditional approach to developing class content is so far removed from students until the day we implement a lesson. If we really want to engage our students, we should think about how to include them in the learning trajectory more effectively. After all, they are by far our most important partners.

Inviting Students In

On my bookshelf at work, I display relics of teaching practice gone by: a stack of lesson-plan notebooks, one for each academic year, spanning many years. Whether we plan our lessons on paper or via digital tools, whether our process occurs mainly alone or collaboratively, most of us have not overtly included students in the act of creating lessons. Even if we do gather feedback from students about what would make their learning process more meaningful, we do not invite students into the planning process as explicitly as we could. It's very much like planning a birthday party without asking the guest of honor what she would like. What if we serve a chocolate cake and she happens to strongly prefer vanilla? What if we hire a clown, and our birthday girl is afraid of clowns? We might not need to go over each exhaustive detail of a party with the honoree, and we do not need to share with our students every piece of how we plan instruction. After all, we know a lot about lesson planning that students do not, and there is only so much they can tell us about *what* we should bear in mind regarding their engagement needs before we work on *how* to execute the learning. However, most of us should be getting more information than we are currently asking for when we plan instruction.

Once we have decided to bring students with us into planning for engagement, what does that look like? The first step is to think of ways to intentionally include them, which can be as simple as asking just a few targeted questions. The most challenging part of this process, other than asking for information from students enough in advance to inform adjustments to lesson planning, is then analyzing and reflecting upon the information we receive. The shared-planning tool in Figure 3.2 contains elements that can be presented in a number of different ways, from a sheet that students fill out manually to an online form.

FIGURE 3.2   SHARED-PLANNING TOOL

LEARNING GOAL: (Teacher fills this part out)
EXAMPLE: *Next week, we will learn how to make line plots on a graph.*

QUESTIONS TO AID IN PLANNING: (Student fills this part out)

- What do I already know about this learning goal, or what words and ideas sound familiar?

- What has helped me learn geometric concepts in the past? Think about class activities (ones I have done before in this class or other classes), how I approach new learning, and what made the experience better.

- In terms of how I learn, what kinds of activities do not work as well? What should my teacher keep in mind to help me as this new learning goal is being introduced?

- How will I know when I have achieved this learning goal, i.e., when I "get it"? If I do not know, what are some ways I know if I "get it" in other subject areas?

- Would I like to volunteer to work with the teacher to plan an activator, class game, or similar? (Please be as specific as possible if you already have an idea. If not, we'll talk.)

While Figure 3.2 demonstrates a scenario in which the teacher is requesting information for a lesson to be given in the following week, this tool can be given to students slightly further in advance. However, it should be noted that students struggle more with big-picture perspectives than we do, and we should not ask questions too far ahead of time. If we do, the class will not be close enough to achieving the previous learning goals, so answers we get from students will not be as applicable or relevant. It is also important to note that we do not need this kind of feedback from students every time we make plans. Sometimes we can ask just one of the questions above, or we could also solicit thoughts after a learning outcome is achieved to inform our future work.

If constantly asking for feedback via questionnaire or similar becomes too repetitive, it is also possible to have structured conversations in class about learning by asking some version of a very powerful question: "What do you think?" One way to help students uncover their thinking about useful engagement strategies is a technique known as "silent discourse." In person, this activity can be done on paper. If students are online, the class can use a shared document. At the top of the page, students write either an open-ended question or a thoughtful comment about their level of interest in or understanding of a particular topic of study. If the class is about to study word problems, a student might write, "Can we learn how to write word problems? I have a hard time understanding some of the language and I usually learn better when I try to do something myself." Students are then directed to pass their papers around, or to read the comments in the online document. As they read, they can add their own replies, check off comments they agree with, and so forth. This proactive method of transparency around how we best engage in new learning does not just accomplish the goal of inviting students into our planning; it also makes our preparation process more visible to the entire class and gives everyone an opportunity to think about how they learn and how their classmates learn. This awareness nurtures a culture of investment and ownership among all students, adding to both their engagement and their willingness to take more initiative.

The Importance of Flexibility

While structure is important, there is a difference between a routine and a rut. If our vision is geared toward class going one way, are we able to open our minds to a different path? For example, if we assign a written response to a documentary the class is watching and a student asks us whether she can create a graphic comic in response instead, are we more inclined to say yes or to refuse? If the latter, what is our reason for maintaining a certain kind of status quo in the details of the work we assign? We often tell ourselves to be more flexible, but making that an actionable step can be challenging. As with any other element of our lesson planning, however, it is possible to work flexibility into our considerations.

In an agile classroom that prioritizes engagement, we provide choices that allow students to work when they are alone, either in school or at home. Think about a typical week of school and how our planning reflects the use of that time. In a more standard model, a teacher assigns work throughout the week with specific due dates and deadlines. Students might work on these assignments in the classroom, or they might do some of it as homework. Either way, we still drive the schedule and the calendar. Suppose, however, that a weekly calendar had more fluidity so that students could choose what to do, choose when to do it, and be given the option to ask for an alternate plan based upon their needs.

Figure 3.3 is a calendar tool that allows students to take individualized variables into consideration. This choice-based calendar provides the overall benefit of responsiveness in real time for students while still providing a big-picture look at where the class is headed over a longer period. Each week, the assignments build upon one another, but the progress is incremental and therefore more manageable. Furthermore, with each passing week, student interaction increases in the form of both peer-review opportunities and discourse-based group activities. Presumably, the assignments detailed in this calendar do not encompass the entirety of how class time is spent, as it is natural for us to check in with students in a whole-group setup or in other ways that might necessitate more overt direction. However, a calendar like the one below provides some freedom

FIGURE 3.3   "YOU-DO-YOU" FLEXIBLE CALENDAR

Below are some options for completing assignments due during the identified time frame. If the dates need to be tweaked, please contact me with an alternate plan via email.

DATE	OPTIONS	ASSIGNMENT
WEEK OF 4/2 (check-in Friday)	**OPTION A:** "Story of an Hour" by Kate Chopin **OPTION B:** Writing practice **OPTION C:** Glossary of multiple-choice terms, letters A–C	▪ Read the short story. ▪ Write paragraphs one and two of the attached prompt. ▪ Create flash cards for each term that is unfamiliar.
WEEK OF 4/9 (check-in Friday)	**OPTION A:** "Story of an Hour" by Kate Chopin **or** choice text (see options on shared classroom document) **OPTION B:** Writing practice **OPTION C:** Glossary of multiple-choice terms, letters A–H	▪ Read and annotate the text for glossary terms. ▪ Peer-review paragraphs one and two; write the next paragraph. ▪ Practice flash cards with a peer; continue building the deck.
WEEK OF 4/16 (check-in Friday)	**OPTION A:** Choice text (see options on shared classroom document) **OPTION B:** Writing practice **OPTION C:** Glossary of multiple-choice terms, letters A–P	▪ Jigsaw discussions on choice text; peer annotation review. ▪ Peer-review with rubric; finish essay draft. ▪ Review unfamiliar terms and do sentence assignment.

both in terms of the schedule and in teacher and student time. In addition, the moves below transcend a physical space, applying to instruction that occurs both near and far.

The You-Do-You calendar in Figure 3.3 is not a complex tool by any means; in fact, it could be a reflection of the assignments that students would complete in a more traditional, less choice-driven classroom setting. However, the presentation of the calendar as a transparent and changeable entity not only allows students to take ownership of their learning; it also has an inherent flexibility. Depending on unpredictable factors that arise, whether with students or with the teacher, this calendar is openly subject to change. With assignments presented in this way, the beauty of a hands-off classroom is realized as each student approaches learning on their own terms with more engagement and buy-in.

Moving Toward Instruction

Thinking once more of my ninth-grade student, his overall investment in the class altered noticeably both in the work he did and in his more focused demeanor during instruction, once we reached a mutual understanding about the texts that engaged him. However, we were not completely out of the woods. It was one thing for me to consider his interests when planning lessons, but quite another to follow through during class time and make sure he was showing mastery of learning outcomes. Now that the student had more options, was he demonstrating gains through improvements in achievement? Did his reading skills grow measurably, or was I confusing his more compliant behavior with academic progress? The only way to find out moves us into the fourth stage of meaningful instruction that results in student growth.

Being a skilled teacher is complex. It involves a lot of moving parts, split-second decisions, and a mindful integration of the four stages of hands-off instruction: an appropriate mindset, relationships that connect to academic goals, student-driven engagement, and the achievement of meaningful instructional objectives. Once we have planned for engagement, we need to make sure to complete the process and go beyond just checking that students are happier; we must also seek measurable results of their efforts. In a classroom that is truly a shared one, students display an agency that transcends the over-interference of their teachers, and that in turn translates into lasting academic achievement.

Words of Wisdom

The key to successfully tapping into student engagement is found in making sure that students play an active role in communicating their needs for engagement. In the *Education Leadership* article "Strengthening Student Engagement: What Do Students Want" (Strong et al., 1995), the authors add an important question in a parenthetical subhead: "And what really motivates them?" The article summarizes and builds upon the findings of several studies on student engagement with these useful takeaway points:

- When students are engaged in class, they attribute that involvement to tasks that tap into their creativity and that allow them to work with others.
- On the other hand, students cited a lack of engagement for tasks that are repetitive, that demonstrate low teacher expectations (i.e., are too simple), and that are compulsory.
- The results of engagement are visible: Students persist in achieving learning goals and show clear enjoyment of the process of completing work.
- Intrinsic motivation is far more effective than extrinsic. As the article references:
  - In *Punished by Rewards*, Alfie Kohn (1995) lays out the prevailing arguments against extrinsic rewards, such as grades and gold stars. He maintains that reliance on factors external to the task and to the individual consistently fails to produce any deep and long-lasting commitment to learning.
- If we want students to be invested in their own learning, we need to build in more clarity around expectations, and criteria for success.
- Students value work that allows them to explore their curiosity and express their ideas with originality.

Questions for Reflection and Growth

As we apply this third stage of engagement to our practice and head into the fourth stage of helicopter-free instruction, consider the following questions:

- What signs of engagement (both verbal and nonverbal) do you look for when you teach? How do you know that some students are engaged, while others are not?
- When you were a student, which classes engaged you the most, and why? Did the teacher do something in particular to increase your engagement, or was there another reason for your interest?
- Consider your process for planning lessons. What small changes could you begin with that might incorporate more student voice into the process?
- When thinking about your planning process, how much of an average lesson reflects teacher talk versus student action? Is there a way to increase the amount students contribute to the class?

The Big Idea

When students are empowered to engage in the content on their own terms, the teacher is able to step back, have more time and space to serve individual needs, and share the responsibility of learning and achievement.

CHAPTER 4

Choice-Based Instruction: The Fourth Stage

One cold, dark wintry morning, I walked into our departmental team room a little before dawn and stopped dead at the sight of one of my colleagues at a computer in her pajamas. She was clearly in the throes of illness, coughing and clutching at a Kleenex box as she frantically typed out lesson plans for a substitute teacher. When I encouraged her to dip into her emergency lesson plans and just go home, she sighed and threw her hands up into the air. "You're right," she said. "They won't learn anything today unless I'm here to help them, anyway. I would stay if I thought I could make it through the day."

It is completely understandable that my colleague was anxious about how student learning could occur without her. However, there is another pathway, one that lets us take sick days when we need to without worry. With tweaks to both lesson design and instructional execution, we can proactively shape our classrooms so that students stay on task without our being physically present.

The Limits of Teacher Presence

The fourth stage of a hands-off classroom relies on instruction that is effective regardless of student or teacher location and proximity. That idea can be challenging to digest; after all, we can become quickly wrapped up in students and in our classroom domains. But the belief that we alone can teach our classes works to everyone's disadvantage. If we instead remove the necessity of our constant presence in the classroom, the result is a situation in which students are ready for learning regardless of whether we are there to supervise each detail. Furthermore, in a culture that increasingly incorporates online learning, it is ever more important to redefine the concept of classroom control.

When we create a classroom that is less teacher-driven, our approach becomes more strategic and proactive. If we think about partially removing ourselves as a classroom focal point, that does not mean we erase ourselves from the equation. Rather, we develop the dexterity to meet a number of ever-shifting demands with students who we intentionally prepare to meet new challenges. This idea probably sounds desirable in theory but unattainable in practice, particularly given the very real and pressing needs students project on a constant basis. To further explore what it looks like to have a learning environment that partially transcends a teacher, let us first compare a static, teacher-directed classroom model to a student-centered dynamic one.

Static or Dynamic Instruction?

Imagine a high school large enough to house its own wing for math classes. Teachers of like teams have been placed in proximity to one another for easier collaboration, and on this particular day, an instructional leader has planned to observe two geometry classes back-to-back to determine how well the same subject area in different classrooms aligns. In this scenario, teachers have coordinated the content of their instruction but not the delivery method. Classes are working to create tables and then graph linear equations, and the instructional leader is eager to see how well students are understanding some of the fundamental concepts of fulfilling this learning objective.

In the first classroom, the teacher stands at the board with a word problem projected onto the screen. Students sit quietly in rows with their notebooks, watching as the teacher demonstrates a word problem. The teacher models the process of converting the results of the word problem into a table and then plots the numbers on the table into points on a graph. As the teacher talks, some students take notes while others simply watch. The more passive members of the class may be paying attention, or they may be off-task with any number of distractions, from texting on their phones to taking a subtle nap. More outwardly active, vocal students are raising their hands to ask questions. The teacher repeats the process of solving the equation with two more word problems before transitioning to the next phase of the class. When the teacher is finished demonstrating the process of graphing a linear equation, she projects a new word problem onto the board. "Your turn," she says.

Students open their notebooks to a fresh page and begin working on the problem. Some of them complete the task quickly and without struggle. Some students stare into space, ignoring the task until the teacher (who is circulating) comes within proximity of their desks. A certain number of students raise their hands and ask for help, having not fully understood the demonstration at the board. One student wanders around the room, offering help to other classmates without being directed to do so. When the bell rings, students gather their notebooks as the teacher says, "We're going to have a quiz on this tomorrow, guys. Be ready."

The instructional leader then heads next door to the second geometry class. Once again, students are learning to graph linear equations. As the class begins, the teacher projects the same series of word problems that her colleague used in the previous lesson onto the board along with an image of a blank table and graph. Students once again have notebooks, but their desks are no longer in rows. Instead, they are arranged in small-group clusters. The teacher has placed half slips of paper marked with an empty table and graph on each set of desks, along with table tents that are marked A, B, or C. These letters correspond with the projected word problems, also marked A, B, or C. In the classroom, there are two groups for each of the letters, making a total of six groups.

The teacher instructs students to look at the word problem their group has been assigned to study. "I know that we have not learned how to do these word problems yet," the teacher says. "In your groups, take about 10 minutes to look at the word problem. On your half sheet of paper, write down some questions about the problem. These questions could be about the situation in the problem, or they could have to do with ways to approach the task. No question is wrong. Just think of as many open-ended questions as you can together, and then we'll come back together as a group."

Students huddle in their groups, looking back and forth between their assigned word problem and the empty table and graph on their half sheet of paper. Slowly, as they adjust to the teacher's request, they begin to talk. One student asks, "What is the connection between the table and the graph?" In another group, a boy frowns as he says, "I don't know what the word 'linear' means." One of his group mates encourages him, responding, "Maybe write that down?" As students talk, the teacher circulates but stays relatively quiet, listening carefully and observing the groups. As she walks, she places large pieces of chart paper on the walls all over the classroom. Each piece of chart paper is marked on top with A, B, or C. On the board at the front, a large digital countdown clock is projected along with the directions, holding both the teacher and students accountable to the stipulated work time.

When the timer goes off, the teacher addresses the class. "Let's take a moment and record our questions on the chart paper. Then, we will discuss." Students write the questions they just developed in groups on the pieces of paper, and the teacher speaks again. "Walk around the class-room and look at the questions," she says. "What are some patterns that we see with the questions? What questions do you wish you had asked? Think about whatever strikes you and be prepared to talk about it." Students move around the classroom in their groups, looking at each set of questions and talking about them as they encounter ideas that resonate.

Throughout the remainder of the class period, the teacher guides the class through looking at the questions, sifting through the various cate-gories they fit into, and encouraging groups to begin approaching finding possible avenues to solving the problem. Before class ends, the teacher explains, "This inductive approach allows you to explore some creative ways to work through making tables and graphing linear equations before we look at some more tried-and-true processes tomorrow. Before you leave, please go back to your half sheet of paper and take a moment to put a star next to a burning question you have about solving these word problems. It can be a question you already wrote, or it can be a new question. Then, give it to me on your way out the door."

In this tale of two classrooms, one model is predictable while the other is divergent. Aside from obvious benefits of a safe environment for risk-taking and questioning that the active student ownership of learning provides in the second model, the structure of the class also enhances its power. The students in that classroom have become accustomed to being listened to and they are comfortable taking risks that put them at the center of acquiring new skills. If the teacher were to be absent, the second group of students would be able to work collaboratively to reach learning outcomes, and they would also believe in their ability to make progress without the constant presence or prompting of an adult. The students in the first group are highly dependent learners who wait for the teacher to direct all of their activities; the students in the second group do not need to see their teacher to know what to do because they have taken responsibility for their own learning. The teacher in the second classroom believes in her students, and she knows that she can learn more about what students need by observing rather than talking.

In the first classroom, both the teacher and the students will remain static, in the same circular pattern, all year long. With each new geometry concept, the teacher will demonstrate a problem on the board and students will either complete the work satisfactorily or struggle. If the latter occurs, the less successful students will most likely be viewed as lazy or less capable, and the teacher will be frustrated at her inability to reach them as the cumulative nature of math instruction places students who are unsuccessful further and further behind. In contrast, responsiveness is an organic part of how the teacher approaches instruction in the second classroom. Student voice is clearly a high priority in both the planning and executing of lessons, and the comfort each student will feel in being heard and in making mistakes results in a classroom that embraces unpredictability and risk-taking.

A classroom free of micromanagement is not driven by a task-oriented approach. Teachers who prioritize learning outcomes and see the bigger picture of what students need to know can more effectively manage the stresses of covering a curriculum. As the class makes collaborative meaning of content, every single learner's perspective is valued. When students see how the power of their voices contributes to the class, the learning community becomes increasingly centered on student efficacy, giving us the freedom to step aside and watch the magic of a student-owned classroom take hold.

Making Way for Student Choice

The first time my children walked, I hovered over them to provide both physical and moral support as they navigated their carpeted play space on unsteady legs. Just as I chose not to let my children learn to walk on hardwood floors (those wipeouts and tears came a bit later), teachers who share new skills want to hold on to students with both metaphorical hands. However, as children develop, become more adept, and adjust to expectations, the process of letting go and stepping back is necessary to ensure that growth occurs, particularly as they age through the secondary school years. The role of a teacher in the first week of school should not look the same as it does in later weeks, once students have adjusted to class rhythms. In a micromanaged classroom, students often adapt to dysfunctional and passive roles in which adults expect them to do very little to advance their own education. In a hands-off classroom, students gain more confidence and learn to be leaders of their own learning without constant adult attention or surveillance.

Stepping back from a model that places a teacher at the fore of all classroom work is hardest for those of us who feel insecure in our ability to manage learning, particularly earlier in our teaching careers. A lot of the narrative bias in education around quiet classrooms equaling productive learning environments drives teachers to be heavy-handed in their approach. I once coached a middle school colleague who began every class with a spelling activity that took up about the first 10 minutes of the period. This practice first caught my attention when I shared a classroom with the teacher and noticed the daily focus on spelling. When I asked him about the connection between the spelling lesson and the learning objective for the day, he said, "They're not really connected. This helps kids come into class and settle down, and then I can start getting into what we learn."

When I visited the class to observe this practice in action, I saw that the spelling work operated as a behavior-management technique with the primary purpose of quieting down the class, and that what came after that initial exercise was nearly a full period of intense teacher control over student learning. Whether students were reading aloud, writing, or even doing a more creative activity, the teacher was in constant motion as he moved from desk to desk, providing nonstop assistance. It was apparent that while this teacher had inventive ideas and a friendly rapport with most of the kids, he did not feel confident that students could come into the room, get to work, and stay on-task without continuous vigilance. As I talked him through some of his more significant challenges with momentum and management, one of the ideas we came back to repeatedly was how to help him restructure his lesson plans to give his students more agency during instruction. That way, among other benefits, he would not feel an unending pressure on his shoulders to drive the class.

Slowly, we began to work on ways to step back. In this teacher's case, he already had a variety of digital and material resources prepared for students. Shifting his approach was therefore more important than changing his course content. An obvious and surface-level fix to the class was to remove the warm-up, trading it out either for a relevant activator that engaged students in thinking about the learning goal, or for a quick framing piece that explained the rationale behind what was happening that day. To create change at a deeper level, I connected this teacher to a colleague in the science department who was known for having success with methods that involved stepping back. In turn, he visited the science teacher's classroom to observe what learning looks like with less teacher interference. When we met to discuss the observation, I could tell that this teacher's entire outlook was different. He referred to his colleague's methods as "revolutionary" and showed a heightened degree of intrinsic motivation to achieve a similar classroom structure. By seeing a dynamic classroom in action, this teacher finally understood how he could step aside. But what did that look like?

He described a room in which the teacher's presence was more subtle, not a glaring focus. When he walked into the room, every single student appeared to be busy and on-task, but they were not all doing the same thing. Some students were reading an article, some were writing the results of lab reports on their laptops, others were reading the science textbook, and two or three kids were engaged in a conference with the teacher about their lab. Periodically, the teacher would begin conferencing with another student, or would pause to get up and check in with the whole class. On the board at the front, a menu of choices for what students could do was posted not just for that day but for the entire unit of study, with dates included. The options for learning also included flexible due dates and a posted list of clear steps for students to follow if they were struggling. The classroom vibe was relaxed, friendly, and open. Nobody seemed to be stressed out, the clarity of expectation was evident, and the class appeared to be running itself. On the surface, everything seemed deceptively effortless.

Learning Menus

To facilitate instruction that minimizes teacher interference, we need tools that provide students with as many choices as possible, and learning menus (also known as choice boards) are ideal for this purpose. Learning menus can be offered during the span of a few weeks or for a longer time over an entire unit. Figure 4.1 is an example of one such menu for a middle school social studies class that is studying the 1920s.

While the example in Figure 4.1 applies to one specific topic, learning menus can be easily adapted for multiple topics and content areas. With the menu, students can make choices based on anything from their perceived strengths (i.e., a love of visual art) to the mood they happen to be in. When we use choice-based boards like the one in Figure 4.1, it is extremely important that students not be forced to do too many of the options. In other words, they might pick three items from the board over a three-week period, but that is about all we would want to ask of them. Otherwise, the self-directed portion of the activity becomes diluted and students lose some of the ownership they might have enjoyed with an added degree of freedom. Furthermore, we might offer students the option of proposing a choice not presented on the learning menu, to give them even more responsibility for how they learn about the content.

FIGURE 4.1 LEARNING MENU (CHOICE BOARD)

Gather five fun facts about this decade that appeal to you.	Write a news item based on a real historical event that occurred in the 1920s.	Create an advertisement for a product that was popular in the time period.	Develop five mock interview questions for a famous figure from the 1920s.
Make a detailed timeline spanning the period of 1920–1929.	**"Roaring Twenties" Learning Menu**		Build a collage with striking images from the time period.
Write a review of a famous piece of art or literature from the 1920s.			Compare and contrast an event from the 1920s with a current event.
Create a piece of visual art that makes a persuasive point about the 1920s.	Design a video-game concept that is built around a historical event from the 1920s.	Write a short script (two-ish pages) for a story that takes place in this time period.	Make a pamphlet or brochure that acts as a "quick guide" to all things Roaring Twenties!

Tools such as a learning menu are a start in building a classroom free of micromanagement, but our constant vigilance and awareness is necessary to keep the ball rolling. Creating a climate of mutual trust is a process that takes a great deal of preparation. That said, the good news is that maintaining a classroom of shared ownership is less challenging than establishing one. Once the teacher and students know what to do, the rest takes care of itself to a degree. The key to keeping a hands-off classroom functional is rooted in the teacher's ability to analyze and reflect upon how students are doing on an ongoing basis. Historically, teacher-directed methods involve a lot of nonclassroom time with either grading or creating lesson plans, often to the extent that teachers feel that the time they spend in class generates more work that needs to be done after hours. In a student-centered model, the teacher has more time to engage in meaningful work both in and out of class. During class, the teacher has freedom to engage with individual students and see what they are doing. For example, in the case detailed above, the science teacher being observed was able to examine student work or provide comments on progress throughout class, which translated into spending less time grading unfamiliar work after class time was over. Essentially, many students and teachers often work in bubbles even if they're in the same room, but dynamic classrooms have the power to lift the veil that covers the learning process for all participants and make thinking visible.

Focused Feedback

As an integral part of stepping back, a "less is more" approach with both student work and teacher feedback accomplishes so much more than piling on more tasks. Let's think about the process of providing feedback to students. We often write exhaustively long comments on student work and hand it back to them, expecting them to read what we have shared and make necessary adjustments. However, that seldom happens. Once they receive returned assignments, students see little point in reading long comments that are difficult to figure out, particularly when the grade is a fait accompli. Suppose that instead of giving students all the information once we hand back their work, we make the criteria for success far more visible from the outset of giving them a task. Figure 4.2 demonstrates how clear and student-friendly criteria for success can be incorporated seamlessly into an assignment.

As we see in Figure 4.2, students are given a checklist that represents the criteria for success along with a choice-based writing assignment. Unlike a rubric, which shows all levels of potential success or failure and anywhere in between (i.e., a 5-to-1 scale or similar), the criteria for success highlight only what students need to do well. The benefit of such a transparent method of sharing expectations is that we show students that there are no secrets to being successful in our class, no codes to crack, and nothing personal about the way we grade. Instead, we share right off the bat what they need to do to meet our expectations. Then, when we grade their work, we can check off the criteria they met and

FIGURE 4.2   CRITERIA FOR SUCCESS

Short Story Assignment

**Please pick one of the three choices below
(or suggest another option).**

Graphic Story	Classic Story	Epic Poem
A visual story representation with comic-book-style panels or similar	*A short narrative written in traditional paragraphs*	*A narrative written in verse, either free verse or metered*

Criteria for Success (Hurray!)

☐ The story is complete (with a beginning, middle, and end).

☐ The story includes attention to detail and sensory language (the five senses) that enhance the plot.

☐ The story uses a balanced mix of dialogue and narration.

☐ There is clear evidence of time and effort (i.e., not a sloppy copy).

☐ The rough draft has been reviewed by two peers using the attached rubric.

☐ The student has adhered to the rules of grammar and mechanics.

☐ If visual components are included, they are aesthetically pleasing (i.e., in color where appropriate and more than rough sketches).

make quick notes about the ones they did not, which streamlines our feedback processes while making them much more effective and clear. The act of openly sharing our expectations while having conversations about what the criteria for success look like before work is submitted for a final grade has the added benefit of building additional trust between teachers and students.

Contrary to what many people perceive, feedback processes do not need to be long or drawn out. Another option for focused feedback is to give smaller assignments or checks for understanding, using these quicker opportunities to gather short feedback that centers on more-specific skills or learning needs. For example, when a class is getting ready to conclude each day, we can ask students to summarize their experiences by writing questions or thoughts on a Post-it Note, sticking it on the wall, and reading one another's ideas as they check off the thoughts of fellow classmates who have similar feelings, questions, or concerns. We might use this time to circulate with students and figure out what to adjust in that moment, or we might find it more helpful to collect the notes and think about what students need going forward. Either way, using methods like the one shared above, often termed an "exit ticket," gauges how the learning is progressing and is an effective way for us to feel more confident about student achievement, both for purposes of course-correction and for being increasingly comfortable with stepping back.

Regardless of how we choose to provide feedback to students, the goal is to be as clear as possible. We might perfectly understand our expectations in our own heads, but students do not have the benefit of being able to see what we think. Therefore, a vital element of maintaining strong relationships and continuing to engage our students so that we can have meaningful instructional outcomes is centered on how we look at student work. As an illustration, when I was in high school, I tended to earn mainly Bs on my essays; my enthusiasm for writing did not blossom until my college years. However, one day I wrote an essay that I felt really good about. When it was returned to me with the usual B grade, I mustered the courage to ask the teacher to explain what I could do better next time, since the grade was not accompanied by any comments or criteria for success. She took the paper back, read it again, and gave me an A with the apology that she had missed a few things in the first reading. The reason

I remember that story is not because I earned what was then a rare high grade; I remember the story because I knew that the teacher had not really read my essay the first time and had instead assigned a grade she was used to giving me. In that moment, I stopped trusting her. As a result, I was less open to any instruction she provided, not to mention less engaged in her class. If we want our students to benefit fully from our hands-off methods that are geared toward their agency, we need to make sure the feedback we provide closes the loop of a teacher-student connection built on trust and mutual ownership.

The Role of Instructional Technology

Several years ago, a rare blizzard descended, closing our large school district for over a week. It was a particularly snowy year and classes were canceled so frequently that teacher stress levels rose as they adapted instruction accordingly. That same year, a new technology had been purchased by the district, one that allowed teachers to assign work and communicate with students remotely with better tools, such as video recordings and recorded voice feedback. Even though we could not meet physically, the week off wound up being less difficult than expected from the perspective of learning disruption. At the time, these innovations were unfamiliar and seemed a heaven-sent way of keeping in touch with students at a distance. Now, thankfully, we live in an age that allows us to integrate technology into our instructional framework in a way that enhances our practice. The key to successfully implementing digital technology is to view it as a complement to a hover-free classroom rather than as a primary driving force.

The process of transcending the teacher in order to achieve a more active student approach is not about the teacher being absent or remote; it is about thinking ahead to what might need to happen by constantly testing the temperature of the classroom and being prepared to make changes on short notice. Furthermore, while we have so many digital tools at our fingertips, we have to apply them wisely so that instruction does not become superseded by technological bells and whistles. Figure 4.3 delineates some of the tools available to us, and how we can use them to supplement meaningful instruction.

FIGURE 4.3   TECH TOOLS

TECH TOOL TYPE	HOW IT WORKS	PURPOSE
ONLINE MEETING (Zoom, Google Meet, Webex, etc.)	Class meetings can occur from anywhere, whether for individuals or for large groups.	Classes can be recorded for absent students, or can meet at times when in-person proximity is not possible.
QUIZ GENERATORS (Quizizz, Kahoot!, Quizlet)	Students engage in a game-like "quiz" about a specific topic of choice.	We can use the data to drive instruction, to create targeted groups, or to reassess as needed.
INTERACTIVE SLIDES OR BOARDS (Nearpod, Pear Deck, Padlet)	Students can respond to questions or content in a variety of creative ways and interact with a shared slideshow.	Immediate feedback can be provided to students and all responses are visible. Furthermore, we get instant results that are easy to analyze.
POLLS OR SURVEYS (Google Forms, Poll Everywhere, Zoom Polling, Doodle Poll)	Teachers can quickly check for understanding with a simple yes/no response.	Shorter, more practical formative assessment methods help us gauge where students are, without anxiety or fanfare.
INSTRUCTIONAL SUPPORTS (Khan Academy, Desmos, etc.)	These free teaching tools (with particular focus on math) allow students to explore content independently.	If differentiation or support is needed, programs like these provide enrichment where needed and applicable.

As the "purpose" column shows, these tools are not a means to an end on their own. Rather, the way we use the tools to gather data about our students and to formulate next steps provides us with clearer direction as we tailor student-centered instruction to meet the needs of the individuals in front of us. Most of these online resources allow for quick, formative assessments that make it so much easier for us to design and execute lessons that keep student voice and learning outcomes at the forefront of all we do.

Structure and Stepping Back: Managing Student-Centered Instruction

No matter what age or stage kids fall into, they want to know what they're in for each day as they enter a class. I observe a great many classrooms and at least a few eager beavers can typically be counted upon to walk in asking, "What are we doing today?" The only way to avoid that interaction is for students to already know what to expect, and in a good way. When it comes to setting up structures and routines that support student-centered classroom practices, intentions matter. In any classroom, effective teachers use the first weeks of school to create expectations that help the class run smoothly; however, many management practices traditionally rely upon a great deal of teacher control, with not as much student involvement in how the class environment is established and maintained. By contrast, routines that proactively plan for student agency are designed to empower students to learn regardless of teacher presence or direct involvement on any given day.

Physical Arrangements

What does a hover-free classroom structure look like? There is most definitely a physical component to setting up a classroom that centers on students and not the teacher. For a long time, education leaders have been tsk-tsking the practice of seating students in rows, and the most commonly proposed solution is to place students in groups. Table groups are a good base model for any given day in class, but a room may need to be set up differently at times to accommodate a variety of possible student choices.

In her popular education blog, blended-learning guru Catlin Tucker (2015) shares a model for learning stations that encourages a more student-centered approach. In the model, students move through four stations: a small-group instruction station, a collaborative project workspace, an online learning area, and a small-group discussion corner. The model emphasizes that students in one room can be physically structured to select options for their learning and to move themselves into relevant areas in the classroom. In this construct, the classroom teacher may play a role in leading small-group instruction, but a student could also fill that role. The stations Tucker identifies can easily be swapped out with other autonomous activities, or to accommodate students who are learning remotely. Teachers can place themselves at any of these stations, or they can exercise the option of meeting with individual students while the rest of the class is engaged. Students might self-select a station, or if need be, teachers can make suggestions about where students work based upon their knowledge of where individuals are in the process of mastering learning outcomes.

While Tucker's model outlines a specific route students follow in a sequence by drawing arrows from one station to the next, removing the arrows is a possible adjustment if students prefer to choose a station based upon their needs rather than on moving in a specific direction. This classroom setup could be in place on a particular schedule (such as designated work days on Tuesdays and Thursdays) or it could be a regular layout. The advantage of the former is that students would learn how to move into flexible formations as needed with the teacher directing very little of that process once everybody knows what to do. Furthermore, there are times when other setups are helpful. For example, one teacher I admire greatly has mastered the art of the Socratic seminar, and for the seminar structure to function with students driving the process, everybody needs to sit in a large circle on the days that a Socratic seminar is planned. No matter what the needs of a class may be, physical setups (both in person and remotely) can get us one step closer to a sustainable, agile classroom.

Routines

Routines are similar to structures in that they provide a degree of familiarity with a teacher's expectations, which is important for students. No matter how much kids may claim to crave unpredictability, they don't want their success to rely on a mysterious target that is visible only to a teacher. Consider the importance of routines particularly when it comes to students who display heightened anxiety when expectations are unclear. I will never forget a girl who came to me early in my career to request that I share my lesson plans with her in advance. At first, I bristled a little as I asked, "Why do you need to know that?" Avoiding eye contact, the student said, "I need to know what's coming so that I can feel better. Don't you like to know what's coming, Ms. P.?" The truth is, I do like to know that, and I learned a lot from what my student shared.

While we think about routines as representing the "how" behind our classroom operations, they are more effective when driven by a clear purpose. Routines do not have to be prescriptive, but they do need to be consistent and grounded in the overall philosophy of a class. In a student-owned environment that seeks to transcend the teacher where appropriate, routines should be built upon the belief that students are equal partners in learning and that they have a shared responsibility for their own learning outcomes. There is no particular formula for setting up routines, but it must be a collaborative process. For example, if the first math class we learned about earlier in this chapter takes a more student-centered approach to solving problems and the goal is for students to understand the context of a word problem before solving it, a possible routine to elevate might be increasing the frequency of student-to-student discourse so that class participants learn to have meaningful conversations about new, challenging concepts.

Even though we likely already have a good idea of which routines would work in a class, presenting students with rationales that categorize the purpose behind each set of routines helps the class move toward a joint understanding of how they work. If the day's purpose is to engage in effective peer review that results in a deeper mastery of a specific skill, then a related routine could be to go through a relevant section of the rubric with a partner in detail before doing anything else. The benefit to couching routines in an overall learning outcome is that the class community will constantly be grounded in mutual desire to own the learning. Furthermore, that overall investment in routines gives teachers the confidence that when their physical presence is not a factor, students will continue to engage in effective learning both in school and at home, not just out of habit, but also from a shared sense of purpose.

Embracing Change

My sick colleague who dragged herself into work to create prescriptive lesson plans was not alone; we have all done the exact same thing time and time again. The question is, do we need to maintain that status quo, or is there a better way? The fourth stage of meaningful, hands-off instruction pulls all our behind-the-scenes work together to create a result that is every teacher's dream. Classrooms with a high degree of student agency may appear fluid and easygoing, but they are thoughtful in their construction. Teachers who seem to have handed a classroom over to students often have more control over the situation than may be apparent; after all, isn't the goal of teaching to empower students to learn on their own and to accomplish objectives in an environment that is beneficial to all learners? As we respond to ever-shifting needs and interests in a world that is increasingly reliant on technology and remote instruction, we create structures that transcend rapidly changing conditions and empower students to learn anywhere, anytime. A busy learning community with engaged, invested participants is therefore a continuing ideal, one that allows us to use time to maximum advantage as we move out of the limelight.

Words of Wisdom

As part of an ongoing study called the Student Agency Project involving a number of classrooms and grade levels, researcher Margaret Vaughn (2019) documents the literature around student agency in "What Is Student Agency and Why Is It Needed Now More Than Ever?" She also provides recommendations for how to move forward with giving students additional ownership during instruction by creating structures to support a more student-centered model. Some of her suggestions include:

- Classrooms in which student agency is evident include higher levels of dialogue and discourse; teachers ask students what they need clearly and often.

- In order to create a culture of collaboration, we must have a clear vision for what our classrooms will look like before we begin instruction.
- Learning should be not merely a transaction but rather a co-constructed endeavor involving both the teacher and students.
- Choice is a key element in creating a student-owned classroom and should be present wherever possible.
- When teaching teams meet to plan instruction, discussions around collaborative structures that support student agency should also be part of the conversation in order to create a vision that centers on student agency.

Questions for Reflection and Growth

- What are some areas of practice that rely heavily on teacher-directed methods? Think about how to move some of that work into the student realm, and what that would look like.
- What is scary or intimidating about the idea of stepping back as a teacher? How can we reframe these feelings and grow in our perception of the teacher's role in a student-owned classroom?
- Thinking about static classroom routines and structures, what words might you use to characterize how students respond to the current state of more teacher-directed models? What is the ideal state for a more student-owned set of routines, and what are some words that describe that ideal state?
- If you could make just one change right away to transcend a teacher-directed classroom culture, what would you decide to do?

The Big Idea

Prioritizing student voice and choice results in the actualization of instructional methods that do not depend on a teacher's micromanagement, ultimately leading to increased student success.

CHAPTER 5

Pulling It All Together: The Four Stages of Hands-Off Instruction

After experimenting with each stage, continuing to work on our practice is a recursive process as we apply theory to action. An ongoing part of teaching is to continuously challenge our mindset, build meaningful relationships with students, plan for engagement, and prioritize choice-based instruction, sometimes in a variety of orders or sometimes (the horror) all at once. How do we know what to look for when the stages come together with real, live people? The answer lies not in the big picture but in the tiny details, which become powerful when they build upon one another. To get a better sense of what that looks like, let's look at two more classrooms side by side.

The Little Details: Hands-Off Teaching in Action

There is something joyful about teaching our classes in a large circle. Circle formations are popular from prekindergarten all the way through higher education. Perhaps we like them because circles naturally lend themselves to eye contact and a little bit of healthy self-awareness when students realize that they are extremely visible not just to the teacher but also to their classmates. While it may seem like there are a limited number of ways to conduct a lesson in a circle and that this classroom setup is inherently student-centered, the following two examples illustrate that a helicopter approach to teaching can exist even in a collaborative seating formation, and that making sure our methods are consciously built for hands-off instruction is about more than just a seating arrangement.

Classroom #1

In my time as an instructional leader, I have been invited to observe countless classrooms. Whenever I receive such an invitation, my usual practice is to drop whatever else I might be doing and visit the classroom. After all, instruction is where our most significant work occurs, and where I can also learn the most from the real experts in education: teachers and students. In one such observation, I visited a class of 30 high school students, all seated in a large circle. The lesson consisted of a discussion about the play A Raisin in the Sun *by Lorraine Hansberry. In front of each student was a list of questions about the assigned scene, as well as a copy of the play. The lesson plan was fairly straightforward: While the teacher sat and occasionally redirected the conversation, students went through every question on the handout and talked about each one before moving on to the next. On the surface, the class looked to be student-directed, and it might have been easy to maintain that perception if not for one or two details.*

One of my tried-and-true practices as a classroom observer involves keeping track of who talks. When I enter a classroom, I make a quick sketch of the seating arrangement. Then, using basic tally marks, I mark down who speaks, and how often. Data has a way of revealing truths that contradict our own gut impressions, and this misalignment between my perception and the reality occurred during the class discussion on A Raisin in the Sun. *Of the 30 students present, only seven of them spoke voluntarily. Of those seven, three dominated the conversation, speaking up multiple times in a back-and-forth exchange of sorts.*

The remaining 23 were silent unless the teacher specifically called on them, and she did so with only four students, when the conversation lagged. Even though many students appeared to be eagerly discussing the play, the tally demonstrated that most of them were not authentically involved in the process.

The other noteworthy aspect of the way this class was structured had a lot to do with the provided handout of questions about the play. As is the case with many of the materials that a teacher generates, students were responsible for talking about the questions on that sheet but were not encouraged to add their own questions. There was no time allocated for additional questions or ideas, nor was there any space on the handout for students to generate their own talking points. As a further constraint, some of the questions were not fully open ended; they had definite yes or no responses, with a "Why?" attached to them. Because the handout was the driving vehicle for class discussion, many of the possibilities around what students could talk about were limited before the class even began. As for students who may not have finished the reading assignment, they had little to say or do except to possibly feel embarrassed about not being able to contribute.

It is important to understand that this classroom teacher was a skilled individual with many years of experience, someone who believed in her students and wanted them to do well. In her mind, she had designed an engaging, student-centric experience, one that allowed class participants to talk to one another in an open-seating setup. Many aspects of this lesson were well conceived and executed. The teacher provided clear guidance for the conversation and sat back for the most part to allow the class to speak. The attention was not on her; it was on her students. There was plenty of evidence to suggest that the teacher was working toward an environment that encouraged students to take academic risks. But I had to ask myself: Was she there yet? Or was there more she could do? The answer lies in a look into another classroom, one in which the teacher made just a few important moves to encourage student agency in a more meaningful way.

Classroom #2

We often realize in our profession that little details can make all the difference. In the second classroom, students were also examining a piece of text and discussing the reading in a large circle, this time for a Civil War unit in social studies class. As in the first classroom, the teacher sat back and mainly remained silent as he jotted down notes about the conversation and occasionally redirected where necessary. However, a couple of minor alterations in his structure created a process that resulted in far more student ownership.

As the instructional period began in Classroom #2, students also received a handout. This time, the first question was open ended and connected to their own experiences: "One of the most heartbreaking aspects of the Civil War was that friends and family often fought against one another. What is a current event or issue that we argue about today that can create conflicts in our personal relationships with others? How do these conflicts influence the bigger world around us?" The question may have been couched in historical context, but every student in the class could respond to the question because it was not solely dependent on course content. The teacher created an accessible entry point to learning, one that invited all students into the conversation without being intimidated by feelings of inadequacy or failure.

In addition to ensuring that all students felt able to make a potential contribution to the conversation, the teacher also had a protocol for sharing thoughts. Before the circle discussion began, each student was given two index cards. These cards represented the number of times they would ideally speak within the time frame of the discussion. Once students made a verbal contribution, they were asked to toss one of their cards into the center of the circle. If students used up both of their cards, they had to stay silent and allow others to speak. In comparison with the first classroom, in which a majority of the 30 students never spoke up, this class had a very different outcome. Of the 26 students in the classroom, all of them spoke at least one time and 19 spoke twice.

All students may have eventually used up both cards, but the bell rang and class ended before that could occur.

Looking at these two circle discussions side by side, what made the second example not just more student-centered but also more conducive to hands-off instruction? If we focus on the differences rather than the similarities between the two situations, the variation in the end result comes down mainly to teacher awareness, particularly during the planning stages of instruction. The first teacher, who planned a clear structure and process for her lesson, may not have thought as much about how a smaller subset of students in the class would take charge of the conversation. Perhaps she realized after the fact that relatively few students actually participated, and felt discouraged by the results of her carefully planned process. The second teacher, on the other hand, was more proactive in his approach. He anticipated that some students would not be as confident in discussing the content and created an inclusive discussion protocol. In addition, he thought about the tendency of some students to dominate a discussion while others hold back and created a method to prevent that from happening, thereby promoting both equitable participation and a whole-class sense of responsibility for engaging in academic discourse with a provided structure.

Sometimes, successfully achieving student ownership is not about how much the teacher plans, or even how skillful the lesson is. Rather, creating a classroom free of micromanagement is more about the intention with which we bring students into a shared learning space, nurture all voices, and continue to plan for maximum involvement. The following anecdote details the experience of a humanities teacher who worked to transform her class from an environment that was highly dependent on her interference to a more dynamic space that allowed her to step back and her students to take the helm.

Story of a Journey

Ms. Cooper is a teaching veteran. She has survived long past the initial three to five years that send many teachers running from the profession, and she has become a teacher who is beloved by students and colleagues alike. From the outside, anyone would describe Ms. Cooper as a creative and visionary teacher. After all, her women's studies elective course, which brings two departments (English and social studies) together with interdisciplinary aplomb, is highly regarded and robustly enrolled. Every year, three classes' worth of juniors and seniors pack into women's studies and there is often a waiting list to get into the course. Ms. Cooper's success is both admired and envied by her fellow teachers, particularly those who continue to struggle to keep their elective classes in the schedule rotation with enough students enrolled.

One day, the school's journalism teacher approaches Ms. Cooper. "I barely have enough kids to keep the newspaper going," the teacher says. "How do you get so many kids to sign up for women's studies?"

This is not the first time someone has asked Ms. Cooper what her secret is, her magic formula. Sometimes she heads off the questions with a joke about luring kids to enroll with high-quality snacks, but today, she sees that the journalism teacher is serious and wants to know the real answer. Ms. Cooper says, "It's really about a journey that I took to get to this point. It was definitely a lot of trial and error."

Ms. Cooper's story begins the same way as many other narratives about a nondynamic class, with certain familiar elements: a dedicated teacher who is feeling burned-out, students who could be doing better but are not, a feeling of sameness from day to day—an educational hamster wheel of sorts. As Ms. Cooper tells it, she hit a teaching wall about 10 years into her career. The zeal of being a fledgling educator had long since worn off and she found herself not just bored but frustrated. In its pilot year, her women's studies course had been received with initial enthusiasm and 30 kids were enrolled, but after the first week 10 of them had already dropped the class. The remaining 20 were rapidly pulling away by spacing out in class or not doing the work, and Ms. Cooper didn't know why. Didn't they want to learn about women's history and literature? Hadn't they signed up for the class voluntarily?

Instead of continuing to wallow in self-pity, Ms. Cooper decided to ask for help from the most valuable source: her students. She distributed a survey in class that asked about their experiences: "Please be frank with me, but also be kind. I'm a human being with feelings, after all. I'm giving you this survey because something isn't working, and I need you to help me figure out how to fix it." Students liked Ms. Cooper. Her class might not be what they had expected or envisioned, but she was friendly and open. She seemed to really care about them. Thus appealed to, they completed the survey with care.

When Ms. Cooper read the results, she found a few patterns. There was no particular issue with *her*, per se; it was more the class structure and her processes. Students thought the content was what they expected it to be but bemoaned the workload: "There is so much reading." Several students also mentioned a lack of interaction: "We don't talk enough about all of the issues. We just watch videos or read articles, write some kind of response, and move on." Finally, there was a pattern in how students perceived the overall vibe: "I signed up because I thought this would be fun, but it feels like English class. Just a lot of reading and writing. Aren't there any projects or activities that we can do?" A similar comment stated: "This doesn't feel like an elective. It feels like work."

At first, Ms. Cooper felt angry as she read the comments. She had poured her heart and soul into designing this class, and to receive this feedback felt personal. After a few minutes and some deep breaths, how-ever, she realized that students had simply done what she asked in sharing their impressions so that she could make some important changes. She needed this information, even (or perhaps especially) if she did not want to hear it. Any resulting actions on her part would have to be transparent so that students would know that their comments were not given in vain. Let's take a closer look at the process that resulted in such a successful course by exploring each stage of Ms. Cooper's journey toward hands-off teaching.

Stage #1: Mindset

First, Ms. Cooper thought about her own "it," or her "why." What had driven her to create this class in the first place? Did the class fulfill her vision and overall goals? In order to self-reflect, Ms. Cooper used the tool below to gauge her mindset. Figure 5.1 includes the questions that Ms. Cooper developed for herself and that, ever since, she has been using before she begins a new school year. As Ms. Cooper tells the journalism teacher she is guiding through her journey, it is helpful to think consciously about our own purpose and how our methods promote student learning before we

FIGURE 5.1   BLANK SELF-REFLECTION (MINDSET)

COURSE TITLE:

THE BIG WHY:

DESIRED OUTCOME(S):

NONNEGOTIABLES:

STUDENT-CENTERED ELEMENTS:

EVIDENCE OF SUCCESS:

ever step into a classroom, so that our mindset reflects a truly student-centered approach.

Ms. Cooper also shows the journalism teacher what a filled-out version of this tool looks like (Figure 5.2).

As the completed self-reflection indicates, Ms. Cooper does not always know how things will turn out. For example, one of her goals is to foster a lasting commitment to women's studies in students, but she will likely not have evidence to measure that goal until (and unless) former students take women's studies courses in college and report back to her about their experiences in higher education. In addition, many of the variables to building a "why" that reduces or eliminates micromanaged teaching depend on how students will react when they are presented with the expectation of shared classroom ownership. Some classes may embrace a model of agency more readily than others. Finally, as Ms. Cooper explains to her colleague, the self-reflection tool is simply a place to start. To ensure that follow-through continues, the process of breaking down and acting upon each element of the tool (Figures 5.1 and 5.2) relies upon moving through the next three stages of building a hands-off classroom environment.

Stage #2: Meaningful Relationships

Getting back to Ms. Cooper's initial experience with building a different kind of classroom in that less-than-successful first year, she was able to diagnose the source of student disengagement and think about how to alter her approach. To see progress, however, Ms. Cooper would need to turn her attention to the relationships she had built with students in those first few weeks of school. By the time she asked for feedback, a third of the students had already dropped the course, and the remaining students were not excited about being there. The damage, while evident, was not a fixed outcome. Ms. Cooper knew that she could repair much of what was broken, and to do that, she zeroed in on how safe students felt taking academic risks in her class.

The first thing Ms. Cooper did was openly acknowledge to the class that she understood that everything had gotten off to a rocky start and make the assurance that she was going to make positive changes. "This is your class, not mine," she said. "You are all choosing to be here instead

FIGURE 5.2 COMPLETED SELF-REFLECTION (MINDSET)

COURSE TITLE:
Women's Studies

THE BIG WHY:
Most of history and literature is told from a male, Eurocentric perspective. I never learned other sides to well-known stories until I pursued them on my own. I want my students to have the opportunity and access that come with hearing voices that are too often silenced.

DESIRED OUTCOME(S):
Students will not only achieve a more balanced view of literary perspective and the historical events that influenced that perspective but will also be able to think more critically and independently about current events or literary works they encounter in the future.

NONNEGOTIABLES:
☐ Student contributions (they bring in materials or works that are significant to them)
☐ Collaborative work
☐ Less "teacher talk"—I don't want to lecture
☐ Transparency, i.e., they know what success looks like, and how to get there
☐ Opportunities for reassessment wherever possible
☐ Flexibility with how assignments are presented as long as they are completed
☐ Consistent feedback (I have to ask for it and implement student suggestions)

STUDENT-CENTERED ELEMENTS:
☐ Varied seating arrangements
☐ Student-led activators
☐ Materials selected not just by me (I want kids to bring in anything relevant)
☐ Emphasis on projects, i.e., learning by doing
☐ Take suggestions for ways to enjoy the process, i.e., "Fun Friday" and so forth

EVIDENCE OF SUCCESS:
☐ Course enrollment and attrition
☐ Engagement, enthusiasm w/ voice data
☐ Academic achievement w/ grade data
☐ Long-term student interest in women's studies, i.e., how many students help promote the course or report back on continuing interest

of in another elective, and you've given me honest feedback about how this could be a better experience. I'm committed to helping you have the class you envisioned, but I will need your partnership. I've placed a shared document on our class webpage and I'm asking you to take just a few minutes now to fill out your own copy and share it with me. This is about the responsibility we all have to own this class. However, you get to decide what that looks like. So on the chart, please take a few minutes to make a contribution. If you are not comfortable with this, please write me a note somewhere on the chart and we can talk privately."

Ms. Cooper knew that unless students had an inviting access point to taking a more active role in the class, they would never be able to tackle bigger risks. For that reason, she began with the chart provided (Figure 5.3), which allowed students to self-identify their preferred methods of class participation and investment. The proposed roles in the left-hand column were accompanied by explanations. For example, the Gamification Guru would find ways to turn class content into a fun review experience with online tools like Kahoot!, and the Activator Mastermind would think of meaningful ways to tie class content into an enjoyable opening activity. Ms. Cooper also asked students for other ideas about how they could contribute and left how often they might do so as a choice.

While some students will understandably hesitate when initially confronted with a tool like this, building agency is a gradual process that takes not just time but also perspective. In Ms. Cooper's class, having each student submit a chart with their ideas filled in gave her information she needed to move forward. For example, a student who wanted to develop a class game only once might be willing to do more if validated the first time, whereas a student who volunteered for many roles as often as possible could help to empower others. As for students who wished to opt out, Ms. Cooper was able to start private dialogues with them, learn more about why they felt hesitant, and use what she learned to tailor instructional decisions about how to bring them into the learning process accordingly as she planned her next move.

Stage #3: Planning for Engagement

With qualitative student voice data in her arsenal, Ms. Cooper explains to the journalism teacher, she was able to move into the planning phase of

FIGURE 5.3   SHARED-RESPONSIBILITY CHART

ROLE	NAME	HOW OFTEN?
Resource Finder (videos, podcasts, articles, you name it)		
Class Discussion Facilitator		
Activator Mastermind		
Gamification Guru		
Question Collector		
Technology Expert		
Feedback Collector		
Other Ideas?		

instruction with a specific focus on student engagement and investment. More importantly, to make sure students saw that she took their contributions and feedback seriously, the information they provided on their charts needed to be worked into instruction with absolute transparency. The upcoming unit of study covered the late 1800s in America. Ms. Cooper's plan had been to read *The Awakening* by Kate Chopin and she still wanted that to be an option, but she also realized that the text might not appeal to all students. As she consulted the information students had provided about how they wanted to contribute, Ms. Cooper began to plan with their involvement in mind. Figure 5.4, a planning tool that incorporates specific student roles, demonstrates the importance of knowing who sits in front of us before committing to finalized lesson plans.

The planning tool in Figure 5.4 may appear complex at first, but it follows a structure that remains consistent from week to week. Student involvement is an essential feature in this planning process to the extent that lessons cannot be fully conceptualized without specific, targeted information about how students will take part. Ms. Cooper did not simply fall into this method of planning; she realized a need to change and experimented with methods that work. Furthermore, Ms. Cooper needed to be willing to constantly tweak her methods to reflect new students, new situations, and newly available technologies. Teaching is an endless process of trial and error, and nowhere is that fact more evident than in how our planning translates into instruction.

Stage #4: Choice-Based Instruction

As Ms. Cooper explains her focus on student engagement through shared responsibility to the journalism teacher, her colleague shows a natural degree of skepticism. "This looks great, but how do you sustain this kind of structure? And does it actually work when you get into class?"

"It works," Ms. Cooper says, "but you have to help students see why *they* want it to work. You also have to be willing to do a little more thinking behind the scenes, but then you have the luxury of time in class to navigate through whatever doesn't play out the way you think it might."

"Can you give me an example?" the journalism teacher asks. "I'm having a hard time picturing this beyond a lesson plan."

Ms. Cooper pulls out her laptop. "Let me talk you through one way

FIGURE 5.4   STUDENT ENGAGEMENT PLANNING STRUCTURE

WOMEN'S STUDIES: WEEK 5

LEARNING OUTCOMES	ESSENTIAL QUESTIONS
By the end of Week 5, students will be able to: ☐ Identify two significant historical events that occurred in America during this time period; ☐ Apply that knowledge to the experience of women of at least two different racial and/or ethnic backgrounds; and ☐ Determine the impact of one of these selected events on a future outcome.	☐ What are some common experiences of all women during this time, regardless of their backgrounds? ☐ Internal vs. external conflict: Which ones emerge as the most significant, and why? ☐ Looking ahead: What events in the past foreshadow our experiences in the present?

	MONDAY	TUESDAY	WEDNESDAY	THURSDAY	FRIDAY
INTRO	*Framing*	*Framing* Activator	*Framing*	*Framing* Activator (Student-Led)	*Framing* Fun Friday Activator!
MAIN EVENT	Intro to essential questions and themes Project ideas Text-choice options Exploration time	Project Q & A via Post-its, gallery walk, discussion Summarizer: "I'm not sure about . . ."	Resource Finder report and share Essential Question small-group exploration Report/ Sharing Summarizer: Exit Ticket	CHOICE DAY: Project outline work time Conferencing Reading time Summarizer: One word	Formative Assessment: Project outline DEAR time, choice of texts Summarizer: Catchphrase of the Week!
WHO	Resource Finder: Drew Question Collector: Anthony	Class Discussion Facilitator: Fatima (topic?)	Gamification Guru: Zoe (quick activity)	Activator Mastermind: Christian	Feedback Collector: Jamie

WHAT				
Desired Outcome: Students have brainstormed ideas for possible project focus. Check for Understanding: Students will submit their initial project ideas.	Desired Outcome: Students will collaborate on a Q & A process to obtain added clarity about the project. Formative Assessment: Use student discussion points to develop formative questions.	Desired Outcome: Each group will present a comprehensive response to one of the essential questions. Criteria for Success: "Exceeds expectations" column on Essential Question rubric.	Desired Outcome: By the end of the class, students will have furthered their progress on class assignments. Check for Understanding: Teacher will conference verbally or check in via email.	Desired Outcome: Students will provide helpful feedback about the progress of their projects. Criteria for Success: Outline meets criteria as specified in Column 5 of the outline rubric.

Notes to Self:
- Remind students of their roles one week in advance
- Do the sign-up for roles for the rest of this unit
- Read and incorporate feedback from Friday into plan where appropriate

students take the lead in my class. This process goes back to when I first started teaching this way, and it's worked so well that I never stopped."

To provide some background, Ms. Cooper says that when she earned her graduate degree, she had a teacher who almost never took the floor. Instead, students in the class selected various themes of study and teamed up to present the content on assigned days in a way that was engaging. Sometimes, admittedly, this strategy backfired; if teams did not work well together, or if the presentations were perceived as a duty to cross off a to-do list, the results were less than ideal. However, Ms. Cooper found herself with a topic she was truly passionate about, and her teammates felt the same way. Thanks to her own positive experience, she decided to try to replicate a successful model of student ownership in her own classroom.

To that end, Ms. Cooper developed student "team-teaching" days. While she could not step back nearly as much as her graduate school professor, a modified version would do quite well for her high school juniors. With a younger audience in mind, Ms. Cooper designed the process detailed in

Figure 5.5, which she made sure to implement at least once in each unit of study.

As the overall rationale states, team-teaching is a valuable learning experience; it is also a practice that students are not usually asked to take part in. In large part, allowing students to act in this role demystifies how teachers build instruction from behind the scenes. When students have the opportunity to team-teach, the empathy and perspective they gain results in a classroom that is far more equally shared among all.

Once Ms. Cooper has shown the journalism teacher these tools and explained their role in her journey to hands-off teaching, she emphasizes that the results of her efforts are gradual and ever-changing. "It's not like

FIGURE 5.5   TEAM-TEACHING PROCESS

RATIONALE:

When we teach, we also learn. Experiencing instruction from a teacher's perspective holds immeasurable value and positions us to be experts on the topic at hand.

GOAL:

Students will demonstrate their own knowledge, understanding, and interpretation of course content through a collaborative delivery of instruction for one class period.

EXPECTATIONS:

- Teams will decide upon a specific coteaching model (team-teaching, parallel teaching, alternative teaching, station teaching, etc.) and include the model in their lesson plan.
- One week prior to the teaching date, teams will submit their lesson plans (using the criteria for success as a checklist) for feedback; the plan will include any concerns or needs.
- Teams will complete individual and group self-reflections after the lesson; the teacher will also write a reflection in addition to completing the rubric and share with the team.
- Each team will meet with the teacher to discuss and reflect upon what went well, what needs work, and what should potentially be taken into consideration for the next team-teaching group.

NEXT STEPS:

Classmates will also provide feedback about the team-teaching experience, which the classroom teacher will use to help guide the process as it continues to evolve and improve.

my class was suddenly popular and all the kids were happy. But it was definitely better, and they appreciated how much I was trying to make it about them. I don't think they had seen that too much before. Word of mouth grew and the class became more popular. We also did an active campaign during registration season to get kids to sign up. But even now, any continuing success comes with a lot of effort. I never take enrollment for granted. Part of it is how much I plan for success, and part of it is how much students are empowered to do."

When it comes to mastering the art of a classroom free of micromanagement, there is no mythical set of strategies that will do the work for us. Ms. Cooper and teachers like her achieve enviable results because of awareness, persistence, and a consistent desire to share their classrooms with students. Furthermore, each teacher's journey is (and should be) different. We all have different styles, different personalities, and different ways of looking at the world. While we share the same desire to serve students, and we should seek to share our successes and helpful strategies, the success of a student-centered classroom will depend on how we apply our repertoire of techniques and strategies to ever-shifting circumstances. For that reason, our creation of classrooms that resist helicoptering must be flexible, independent of specific location or situation, and fully embraced, not in spite of constant change, but rather because of it.

Combining the Stages

Cognitive studies hold that multitasking is an impossibility. However, of all the people who claim to do many things at once, teachers are probably the closest to actually achieving that ideal. In a profession that requires us to make what multiple sources estimate is 1,500 decisions per day, the luxury of doing just one thing at a time is unrealistic at best. From a practical standpoint, we need to make the very complex demands of instruction work not just seamlessly but effectively. To that end, we can combine the four stages of hands-off instruction into one cohesive process as we move toward experimenting with a new approach.

Working recursively through the four stages and adjusting our methods to step away from micromanagement, it is helpful to organize our ideas around how theory plays into practice to better move us from thinking to action. The "Your Job, My Job, Our Job" organizer (Figure 5.6) helps us to think about how teachers and students work as individual entities as well as together in all stages of hands-off instruction. To use this tool, it is advisable to have a bigger-picture learning target or goal in mind. The chart is designed for us to go beyond planning a specific daily lesson; rather, this organizer (shown in Figure 5.6 both blank and filled out) helps us to make far-reaching, clear decisions about the contributions we make to our classes, those that students make, and the factors that influence shared ownership of learning.

Figure 5.6 allows us to combine the four stages of hands-off teaching in a way that is practical and user-friendly. Our belief in student efficacy is demonstrated throughout the "Your Job" column, reflecting a mindset free of helicoptering. Students are clearly seen both as drivers of their learning and as facilitators, working both collaboratively and individually to reflect upon their own progress and to share ideas with their fellow

FIGURE 5.6 "YOUR JOB, MY JOB, OUR JOB" ORGANIZERS (BLANK AND FILLED OUT)

DIRECTIONS:

- Think about an upcoming unit of study. Consider the desired learning outcomes as well as the processes or elements that are needed to facilitate the successful achievement of those outcomes.
- Using the chart designations below, clearly identify how each role plays a part in the learning goals. "Your Job" is for students, "My Job" is for the teacher, and "Our Job" bears shared ownership.

LEARNING OUTCOME:

YOUR JOB	MY JOB	OUR JOB

Your Job, My Job, Our Job: Mindset Organizer

DIRECTIONS:

- Think about an upcoming unit of study. Consider the desired learning outcomes as well as the processes or elements that are needed to facilitate the successful achievement of those outcomes.
- Using the chart designations below, clearly identify how each role plays a part in the learning goals. "Your Job" is for students, "My Job" is for the teacher, and "Our Job" bears shared ownership.

LEARNING OUTCOME:

Students will develop the skill of elaborating on their writing by adding details (both sensory and otherwise) to writing assignments consistently over the course of this unit.

YOUR JOB	MY JOB	OUR JOB
Have a journal at the ready every class period	Create a list of simple statements to use as an ongoing activator	Participate actively, not passively; listen to one another and balance verbal/nonverbal contributions
For all collaborative work time, track the contributions of all group participants using the provided tool	Develop collaborative tools to help students track their involvement and engagement during group work	Determine group progress toward the learning outcome with analysis and reflection
Pull "Before" and "After" writing-sample pieces for one-on-one conferencing	Schedule and design teacher-student writing conferences to examine progress over time with the learning outcome	Work together with the writing samples to look for areas of progress as well as possible areas for improvement in relation to learning outcome
Find samples of descriptive writing from outside sources to share with the class	Find additional samples of descriptive writing from outside sources to share with the class	Critique the samples together according to criteria for success; determine what makes the samples successful (or not)

students. With ample means to check in with students one-on-one as well as in groups, the chart showcases a teacher who has set aside time for meaningful relationship-building. There is also evidence of clear planning for engagement that translates into lessons that are jointly and explicitly owned by both teachers and students.

Most importantly, the "Your Job, My Job, Our Job" organizer showcases the simplicity with which we can implement a hands-off approach. The art of teaching is certainly complex, but we do not have to make the process even more difficult with endless bells and whistles. Any tools we decide to use are as powerful as we choose for them to become in their implementation, and it is our responsiveness and agility that provide the ideal results we seek. Each new year, new unit, or new lesson provides us with opportunities to continue experimenting with what works best for our students. With an eye toward constantly developing our craft without overwhelming ourselves, we can go so much further with the gradual increase in student agency and partnership.

Putting It All Together

When I was a child, Magic Eye images were all the rage. Cartoon pages in newspapers and puzzle books in the library contained pictures that looked like nothing in particular but that were designed to form a specific image when viewed out of focus. Eager to join in the fun, I tried over and over again to see the hidden pictures. Many years and even more attempts later, I finally gave up. The pictures just never crystallized, and I still wonder if there is anything behind all the jumbled patterns and colors, or whether the world is having a laugh at my expense.

Epiphanies are rare, and they are precious. Some of us never see things that others do, but we make our own meaning of the world around us. My own journey, shared in the first chapter of this book, details my gradual awakening to a teaching style that puts the spotlight where it belongs—on students. Throughout this book, my goal has been to share the four stages to accomplishing instruction without micromanagement (more accessible, I hope, than a Magic Eye puzzle) and make this teaching approach transparent to the people who are closest to the work: my fellow teachers. As with every puzzle, or every challenge, achieving a classroom that is a clear vehicle for student agency is not only an ongoing process but one that requires our constant vigilance and adjustment. But isn't that one of the many glories of teaching? The opportunity to start afresh, again and again, and get it just a little more right each time?

As you embark upon your own journey to a hands-off classroom, I encourage you to experiment with the techniques and ideas shared in this book, to make them your own, and to collaborate with others. Share successes, but also share the frustrations and mistakes; these missteps represent the highest level of learning if we can just maximize what we learn from our low points as well as our high ones. And through it all, from the days where instruction completely bombs to the days it feels like the most effortless joy imaginable, we can continue to share our feelings openly with our students, who will respect us all the more for our humanity, for our skill set, and for our love of what we do.

The Big Idea

The consistent elevation and implementation of the four stages to achieving a hands-off classroom results in a fulfilling and successful journey to the shared ownership of learning for both teachers and students.

References

Fagell, P. (2019, August 20). How to talk to your middle-schooler (so they might actually listen to you). *The Washington Post*. https://www.washingtonpost.com/lifestyle/on-parenting/how -to-talk-to-your-middle-schooler-so-they-might-actually-listen-to -you/2019/08/19/941fec26-a4c2-11e9-bd56-eac6bb02d01d_story.html

Garcia Mathewson, T. (2019, March 27). How to unlock students' internal drive for learning. *The Hechinger Report*. https://hechingerreport.org/ intrinsic-motivation-is-key-to-student-achievement-but-schools-kill-it/

Garrison, D. R., Anderson, T., & Archer, W. (2000). Critical inquiry in a text-based environment: Computer conferencing in higher education. *The Internet and Higher Education, 2*, 87–105.

Jackson, R. (2018). *Never work harder than your students and other principles of great teaching* (2nd ed.). ASCD.

Plotinsky, M. (2019, October 3). The incredible benefits of letting students drive their own learning. *EdSurge*. https://www.edsurge.com/ news/2019-10-03-the-incredible-benefits-of-letting-students-drive-their -own-learning

Reinhart, S. (2000). *Never say anything a kid can say!* National Council of Teachers of Mathematics. https://www.nctm.org/Publications/ Mathematics-Teaching-in-Middle-School/2000/Vol5/Issue8/Never-Say -Anything-a-Kid-Can-Say!/

Strong, R., Silver, H. F., & Robinson, A. (1995). Strengthening student engagement: What do students want. *Educational Leadership, 53*(1), 8–12. http://www.ascd.org/publications/educational-leadership/sept95/vol53/num01/Strengthening-Student-Engagement@-What-Do-Students-Want.aspx

Tucker, C. (2015, July 20). Create small learning communities with the station rotation model. *Dr. Catlin Tucker.* https://catlintucker.com/2015/07/creating-small-learning-communities-with-the-station-rotation-model/

Vaughn, M. (2019). What is student agency and why is it needed now more than ever? *Theory Into Practice, 59*(167). https://doi.org/10.1080/00405841.2019.1702393

Index

Note: Italicized page locators refer to figures.

academic freedom, critical thinking and, 8
academic risk-taking, in safe environment, 22, 25, 26, 30, 37, 61
achievement
  lasting, student agency and, 54
  sharing responsibility of, 55
Activator Mastermind
  in shared-responsibility chart, 87, *88*
  in student engagement planning structure, *90*
activators, developing or facilitating, xv
active learning roles, student investment in, 40–42
adolescent students, voice and choice for, xxii
agency. *see* student agency

agile classrooms, engagement and, 51
agility, xvi, xxiii
answers in class, validating, 25
assignments
  criteria for success options, 66, *67*
  list of expected criteria in, *35*
autonomous activities, 72
autonomy of students, celebrating power of, 26
Awakening, The (Chopin), 89

backing off, 2
beliefs
  changing, 18
  current, challenging, 14–15, 18
  translating into action, 19
brainstorming, mindset shifts, 15

calendars
  choice-based, 51, *52*, 53
  weekly, 51
  "You-Do-You," *52*, 53
change
  embracing, 74
  resistance to, 15
choice, xvi
  in agile classrooms, 51, 53
  student-owned classrooms and,
    75
choice-based, hands-off instruction
  (the fourth stage), xviii, 57–75
  big idea for, 75
  embracing change, 74
  focused feedback, 66, *67*, 68–69
  journeying toward hands-off
    teaching, 89–93
  learning menus, 64–66, *65*
  limits of teacher presence, 58
  making way for student choice,
    62–64
  managing student-centered
    instruction, 71
  physical arrangements, 71–72
  prioritizing, 77
  questions for reflection and
    growth, 75
  role of instructional technology,
    69, *70*, 71
  routines, 72–74
  static *vs.* dynamic instruction,
    58–62
  words of wisdom, 74–75
choice-based calendars, 51, *52*, 53

choice boards (learning menus),
  64–66, *65*
Chopin, K., 89
circle formations, 77–81
Class Discussion Facilitator
  in shared-responsibility chart, *88*
  in student engagement planning
    structure, *90*
classroom community, pandemic
  and rapid evolution of, xvii,
    xxii
classroom management, micromanagement *vs.*, 3. *see also*
  hands–off classroom
cognitive presence, online learning
  and, xxii
collaboration
  creating culture of, 75
  hover-free teaching and, xx
collaborative project workspaces, 72
commensalism, 22
Community of Inquiry framework,
  xxii
concurrent instructional models,
  prevalence of, xvii
content, student engagement with,
  on their own terms, 7, 39–42,
    48, 53–54, 55
continuing education, xix
control
  daily agenda and, 9
  fear of loss of, 3
core teaching beliefs, exploring
  new set of, xiv
COVID-19 pandemic, xxii, 3, 4

creativity, student engagement and, 54

criteria for success

rubrics *vs.,* 66

short story assignment, 66, *67,* 68

critical thinking, academic freedom and, 8

culture of collaboration, creating, 75

current beliefs, challenging, 14–15, 18

curriculum goals, relationship growth in conjunction with, 32

daily agenda, mutual trust and, 8–9

deadlines, 45, 51

deeper relationships

building, strategies for, 29–30, *31–32*

effective educational space and, xviii

fostering, 22

see also reframing relationships (the second stage)

Desmos, *70*

details dump activity, *33*

digital technology

leveraging, xxi

role of, 69, *70,* 71

disengagement in students, diagnosing source of, 85

distance-learning models, xxi, xxii

Doodle Poll, *70*

due dates, 5, 8, 45, 46, 51

dynamic instruction, static instruction *vs.,* 58–62

dynamic planning guide, 46, *47*

empowering

all learners, 39–42

without constant oversight, 42

engagement (the third stage)

active learning roles and, 40–42

agile classrooms and, 51

big idea about, 55

empowering all learners and, 39–42

focused feedback and, 68

journeying toward hands-off teaching, 87, *88,* 89

learning menus and, 66

moving to investment from, 39–55

planning for, xviii, 43, 44–46, *47,* 48

prioritizing, 77

questions for reflection and growth, 55

transparency and, 50, 53

visible results of, 54

winning students over, 42–44

words of wisdom about, 54

engaging activities, connected to daily content objective, *35*

"exit tickets," 68

expectations

building clarity around, 54

routines and, 73

sharing, 66, 68

student-centered instruction and, 71

external motivation, 42, 43

extrinsic rewards, 54

eye contact, circle formations and, 77

Fagell, P., 23

feedback, *35*, 46, 48, 50, 82–83, 85

about team-teaching experience, *92*

focused, 66, *67*, 68–69

Feedback Collector

in shared-responsibility chart, *88*

in student engagement planning structure, *90*

flexibility

importance of, 51, 53

You-Do-You calendar, *52*, 53

flexible activator ideas, *33*

flexible mindset, 44

focused feedback, 66, *67*, 68–69

focus groups, xv

Gamification Guru

in shared-responsibility chart, 87, *88*

in student engagement planning structure, *90*

geometry class scenario, static *vs.* dynamic instruction in, 58–62

global pandemic. *see* COVID-19 pandemic

Google Forms, *70*

Google Meet, *70*

grades and grading, 42, 43, 46, 54, 65, 66, 68–69

group conversation, *35*

growth, letting go and, 62

hands-off classroom

big idea for, 97

choice-based instruction, fourth stage in, xviii, 57–75, 89, *90–91*, *91–93*

dynamic class community and, xvii–xviii

from engagement to investment: third stage in, xviii, 39–55, 87, *88*, 89

learning to believe in, 5

mindset shifts: first stage in, xviii, 1–20, 83, *84*, 85

ownership of learning in, 53

putting it all together in, 96–97

reframing relationships: second stage in, xviii, 21–37, 85, *86*, 87

writing class scenario, 5–6

hands-off instruction

combining the stages in, 93–94, *94*, *95*, 96

gradual shift to, xvii–xviii

in two classrooms, the little details in, 77–81

see also choice-based, hands-off instruction (the fourth stage)

"hands-off" stages, birth of, xvi

hands-off teaching, power of, xxiii

Hansberry, L., 78

helicopter parents, xxi

helicopter teaching, xxi, 8, 93

in collaborative seating formation, 78–79

letting go of, 1–4

looking for possible indicators of, 9, *10*

see also micromanagement

higher-order thinking questions, asking, 36

hover-free instruction, four stages of, xvii–xix

    choice-based, hands-off instruction, xviii, 57–75, 89, *90–91,* 91–93

    deeper relationships, xviii, 21–37, 85, *86,* 87

    mindset shifts, xviii, 1–20, 83, *84,* 85

    planning for engagement, xviii, 39–55, 87, *88,* 89

    see also hands-off classroom

"hover-free" stages, birth of, xvi

hypercontrol, leaving behind, xvii

hypervigilance, xxi

implicit bias, awareness of, xiv

in-person instructional models, xvii

instructional supports, *70*

instructional technology, role of, 69, *70,* 71

instructional time, virtual classes and loss of, 4–5

interactive slides or boards, *70*

intrinsic motivation, 39, 41, 43, 46, 63

investment

    in learning, 40–42, 50, 53, 54

    moving from engagement to, 39–55

inviting students in, 48, *49,* 50

Jackson, R., 19

Jamboard, *31,* 37

Kahoot!, *70,* 87

Khan Academy, *70*

Kohn, A., 54

learners, empowering, 39–42

learning

    advance planning for engagement and, 46

    creating accessible entry points to, 80, 87

    in hands-off classroom, 53

    investment in, 40–42, 53, 54

    long-lasting commitment to, 54

    power of student autonomy in, xviii

    sharing preferences for, 9

    sharing responsibility of, 55

    structured conversations about, 50

    styles of, accessible topics and, 43

    teachers as collaborative designers of, 45

    virtual, xxii, 4

learning menus (choice boards), 64–66

    adapting for multiple topics, 64

    mutual trust and, 65

    "Roaring Twenties," 65

learning outcomes, couching routines in, 73–74

learning stations, 72

lesson planning
  dynamic planning guide for, 46,
    47
  factoring students into, 46, 48
  targeting relationship-building
    in, 29
letting go, growth and, 62
Lewis, M., 44
lifelong learners, planning classes
  for students as, 44
Love, Love Not activity, *33*

Magic Eye images, 96
Mathewson, T. G., 42
micromanagement, 1–4
  achieving classrooms free of, 44,
    96
  classroom management *vs.*, 3
  community dynamic free of,
    xviii
  looking for possible indicators of,
    9, *10*
  moving to trust from, 8–9, 11
middle-schoolers, level of distress
  experienced by, 23
mindset
  continuously challenging, 77
  as powerful determinant of suc-
    cess, 1
mindset myths chart
  how to use, *16*
  sample of responses to, *17*
mindset quiz, 11, *12,* 13
mindset shifts (the first stage),
  xviii, xxiii

additive *vs.* repetitive approach
  to, 18
big idea about, 20
brainstorming, 15
celebrating student autonomy
  with, 20
challenging current beliefs,
  14–15, 18
examining the meaning of
  urgency, 4
gaining momentum for, 18–19
journeying toward hands-off
  teaching, 83, *84,* 85
laying the groundwork for, 11, 13
letting go of helicopter teaching,
  1–4
mindset myths chart activity,
  16–17
moving from micromanagement
  to trust, 8–9, 11
questions for reflection and
  growth, 20
rethinking control, 4–8
words of wisdom about, 19–20
minimum competency, moving
  past, 45
Moneyball, 44
motivation
  external, 42, 43
  intrinsic, 39, 41, 43, 46, 63
multitasking, teaching and, 93
mutualism, 22
My Favorite Mistake strategy,
  description, virtual twist, and
  purpose of, *31*

Nearpod, *70*

"Never Say Anything a Kid Can
Say!" (Reinhart), 36

*Never Work Harder Than Your
Students and Other Principles of
Great Teaching* (Jackson), 19

new teachers, helicopter teaching
and, 1–3

One Thing activity, *33*

One Word strategy, description,
virtual twist, and purpose of,
32

online learning
classroom control and, 58
three "presences" for, xxii

online learning areas, 72

online meetings, *70*

opening warm-ups in class, 29–30

overplanning, xvi

ownership
awareness and culture of, 50
in hands-off classroom, 53
sharing, 34, 97

Padlet, *32, 37, 70*

parasitism, 22

passive roles, in micromanaged
classrooms, 62

Past Me, Present Me strategy,
description, virtual twist, and
purpose of, *31*

Pear deck, *70*

physical arrangements, in hover-free classrooms, 71–72

Picture is Worth... activity, *33*

Pierson, R., 9

Poll Everywhere, *70*

polls, online, *70*

presence of teacher, limits of, 58

presentation outlines, fluid, 45, 46

professional growth, building self-
run classrooms and, 18

Punished by Rewards (Kohn), 54

purpose, routines and, 73–74

Question Collector, in shared-responsibility chart, *88*

questions, soliciting several
answers to, 36

quiz generators, *70*

Quizizz, *70*

Quizlet, *70*

Raisin in the Sun, A (Hansberry),
78

rapport building, 28

reading skills, improvement in, 41

redirecting students, 24

reframing relationships (the second stage), 21–37, 42, 96
before *vs.* after, 34, *35*
big idea about, 37
focused feedback and, 68
journeying toward hands-off
teaching, 85, *86,* 87
prioritizing, 77
questions for reflection and
growth, 36–37
trust before teaching, 26–29

reframing relationships (*continued*)
  unspoken relationship-building, 25–26
  words of wisdom about, 36
Reinhart, S., 36
relevance, peak, planning classes for, 43
reluctant students, reaching, 21–25
remote learning models, xxi. *see also* online learning; virtual learning
research gap, looking to higher education, xxi–xxii
resistance to change, 15
Resource Finder, in student engagement planning structure, *90*
responsibility, giving back to students, xxiii. *see also* shared-responsibility chart
responsiveness, student voice and, 61, 62
"Roaring Twenties" learning menu, *65*
routines, 72–74
  consistent, 73
  expectations and, 73
  purpose and, 73–74
  structures and, 72
rubrics, criteria for success *vs.*, 66

safe environment
  academic risk-taking in, 22, 25, 26, 30, 37, 61
  opening warm-ups and, 29–30

self-awareness, circle formations and, 77
self-efficacy, 28
self-exploration
  through reflection, 14
  tools, xv
self-reflection
  building self-run classrooms and, 18
  on mindset (blank), *84*
  on mindset (completed), *86*
  mindset quiz, 11, *12, 13*
self-run classrooms
  achieving, 4
  building, professional growth and, 18
  changing to, incremental process in, 18
  first priority in, 7
  questions for reflection and growth, 20
shared ownership, creating classroom of, xviii
shared-planning tool, 48, *49*
shared-responsibility chart, 87, *88*
short story assignment, criteria for success, 66, *67,* 68
sick days, 57
"silent discourse" technique, 50
slowing down, xvi, xxii
small-group discussion corners, 72
small-group instruction stations, 72
social presence, online learning and, xxii
Socratic seminar, *35, 72*

static instruction, dynamic instruction *vs.*, 58–62
stepping back, xv, 6, 7, 8
sticky notes, attaching to web boards, *31*, 37
"Strengthening Student Engagement: What Do Students Want" (Strong et al.), 54
structure(s)
  collaborative, 75
  routines and, 72
student agency, xvii, xxii, 1
  encouraging, xv, 79–81
  engagement with content and, 7
  gradual increase in, 87, 96, 97
  hands-off teaching and, xxi
  lasting academic achievement and, 54
  positive teaching energy and, xxiii
  restructured lesson plans and, 63
  routines and, 73
  thoughtful classroom construction and, 74, 75
Student Agency Project, 74
student-centered instruction, managing, 71. *see also* student agency
student-centered learning, xvi
student-centric models, xv
student choice, making way for, 62–64
student efficacy, focus on, 62
student engagement planning structure, *90–91*

students
  believing in, as people and as learners, 30
  giving responsibility back to, xxiii
  inviting into planning process, 48, *49*, 50
  ownership and, xviii, 13
  reluctant, 21–25
  who act out, 22
  who slip through the cracks, 21–22
  winning them over, 42–44
  see also student agency; teachers
student "team-teaching" days, developing, 91, *92*, 93
student voice, xvi, 75
surveys, *35*, *70*, 82–83
symbiosis, three kinds of, 22

table groups, 71
talking less, xv, 36
teacher presence
  limits of, 58
  online learning and, xxii
teachers
  as collaborative designers of learning, 45
  "cool" or popular, 27
  see also students
teaching
  as an art, xix
  as a verb, xix–xx
  see also helicopter teaching
teaching methodology, release of helicoptering and, 11

teaching role, continual shifts in, xxiii

team-teaching process, *92*

technology, role of, 69, *70*, 71

Technology Expert, in shared-responsibility chart, *88*

theory *vs.* practice, xix–xxi

time constraints, adjusting, 45

tracking, xiii–xiv

transparency, engagement and, 50, 53

trust, 7, 8

  before *vs.* after: reframing relationship building, 34, *35*

  broken, 23

  collective power of classroom community and, 15

  eroded, 69

  going beyond surface level, 30

  learning menus and climate of, 65

  moving from micromanagement to, 8–9, 11

  mutual, 36, 37

  relationship-building and, 23, 24, 25, 26, 42

  before teaching, 26–29

Tucker, C., 72

Tweet It! activity, *33*

20 questions, *33*

Universal Design for Learning (UDL), xvi

University of Alberta, xxii

urgency, examining the meaning of, 4

validating student contributions, Jennifer's Story, 23–25

Vaughn, M., 74

verbal contributions, in circle discussions, 78–81

virtual classes, loss of instructional time and, 4–5

virtual instructional models, xvii

virtual learning, global pandemic and, xxii, 4

virtual teaching, lack of research about, xxi

virtual tools

  Jamboard, *31*, 37

  Padlet, *32*, 37

"warm demander," xv–xvi

Webex, *70*

weekly calendar, fluidity in, 51

well-being, release of helicoptering and, 11

"What if?" question, about course content, *33*

"What Is Student Agency and Why Is It Needed Now More Than Ever?" (Vaughn), 74

"You-Do-You" flexible calendar, *52*, 53

"Your Job, My Job, Our Job" organizers

  art of teaching and, 96

  blank, *94*

  filled out, *95*

Zoom, *70*

Zoom Polling, *70*

About the Author

Miriam Plotinsky is an author and instructional specialist who addresses challenges in both teaching and leading across schools with a wide range of differentiated needs. A strong advocate for student-centered learning, she provides coaching and professional development for teachers and administrators. Plotinsky is widely published in *Education Week, Edutopia, ASCD Express, The Teaching Channel, EdSurge, K–12 Talk,* and *Education World.* Plotinsky is also a National Board Certified Teacher with additional certification in administration and supervision. She lives in Silver Spring, Maryland with her husband and three children, and can be found on her website at www.miriamplotinsky.com.